BEYOND THE CHALKBOARD:

A FAITH-FUELD GUIDE FOR TEACHERS

ANTHONY DAYSE, PH.D.

ISBN: 979-8-9902680-0-5

Publishing By: DemiCo National, LLC

www.DemiCoNational.com

Acknowledgements

To my beloved wife, Maribel, and my two wonderful children, Maria and Anthony, your love, support, and understanding have filled my life with immeasurable joy and happiness. This book is as much yours as it is mine. Thank you for being my constant inspiration and motivation.

-Anthony

Chapters At-Large

Chapters Overview

Chapter 1 discusses the idea that teaching is not just a job but a calling from God. Exploring the spiritual aspects of being an educator. Chapter 2 addresses the everyday challenges of managing classroom dynamics. Sharing practical tips and strategies for maintaining a positive learning environment. Chapter 3 explores the challenges of interacting with parents who may have concerns or issues. Offering guidance on maintaining positive and constructive communication.

Chapter 4 discusses the importance of collaboration and teamwork among educators. Providing insights on dealing with challenging relationships among colleagues. Chapter 5 Acknowledges the times when teachers may question their purpose. Offering encouragement and strategies for rediscovering meaning in their work. Chapter 6 explores ways to incorporate faith into teaching practices. Discussing the role of spirituality in providing a sense of purpose and fulfillment. Chapter 7 provides stories of teachers who have made a significant difference in students' lives.

Providing guidance on how educators can inspire and empower their students. Chapter 8 addresses personal challenges that teachers may face outside the classroom. Offering support and encouragement for overcoming difficulties through faith. Chapter 9 highlights moments of triumph and success in teaching. Encouraging teachers to celebrate their achievements and recognize the positive impact they have. Chapter 10 Emphasizes the ongoing process of personal and professional development. Providing guidance on maintaining a strong connection to faith throughout one's teaching care.

CHAPTER 1:

The Calling: Embracing the Teaching Profession as a Divine Calling

Meaning and spiritual dimensions of teaching...

Reflecting on the journey that brought me to perceive teaching as a divine calling, I'm reminded of vivid childhood moments that foreshadowed my future role. As a child, I would immerse myself in games of 'school' with my peers and little did I know that these innocent play sessions held the seeds of a profound revelation. One particular day stands out—the moment when a seemingly ordinary child engaged in this imaginative play, embodying the role of a teacher, unknowingly set the stage for a sacred calling.

Picture this; a group of children gathered in the warmth of their innocence, reenacting the dynamics of a classroom. In the midst of laughter and make-believe lessons, I felt a profound connection to the act of teaching, as if an invisible force was gently guiding my path. It was a whisper from the divine, a subtle revelation that hinted at the sacred purpose awaiting me.

Looking back, I realize that God, in His infinite wisdom, used the canvas of child's play to sketch the outline of my future vocation. This isn't a universal truth, but it underscores the possibility of divine preparation, an intricate weaving of our destinies long before we comprehend our life's purpose.

Teaching ceased to be a mere profession—it became a calling, a sacred duty entrusted to me by divine design. Through these early, playful moments, God planted the seeds of purpose in the soil of my heart, and as I nurtured them through the years, they blossomed into a profound understanding: that teaching is not just a job, but a calling crafted by the hands of a higher power. It is this realization that has infused my journey with meaning, purpose, and a sense of the divine in every lesson taught and every life touched.

Integrating your faith into your daily teaching practices…

Incorporating my faith into daily teaching practices is not just a deliberate choice but a fundamental aspect of how I approach education. I firmly believe that children are sponges, absorbing not only the academic knowledge we impart but also the values and virtues we exhibit. Every interaction in the classroom is an opportunity to illuminate their minds with a positive light.

For instance, the way I carry myself, the language I use, and the decisions I make in the classroom all stem from the wellspring of my faith. It is not merely about preaching or explicitly discussing religious principles; it's about embodying those principles in my demeanor and actions. A simple example is the power of kindness—treating each student with respect and compassion, mirroring the teachings of empathy, and understanding that my faith encourages.

Faith, in my view, is not a separate entity confined to a particular time or place; it is interwoven into the very fabric of my teaching. It is reflected in the smiles I share, the encouragement I provide, and the moments of solace I offer when a student is facing challenges. My belief system shapes not only my attitude but also influences my choice of words, expressions, and gestures in the classroom.

Moreover, faith acts as a silent but powerful guide in cultivating positive confidence. The confidence derived from faith is not just about personal assurance; it's a beacon that radiates assurance to my students. They can sense when a teacher is grounded in a positive and uplifting belief system, and this, in turn, fosters a conducive learning environment.

Integrating faith into teaching is a holistic approach—it's about infusing the learning space with an ethos of love, respect, and moral integrity. By aligning my faith with my actions, I hope to not only educate minds but also nurture hearts, fostering an environment where every child feels seen, valued, and inspired to grow not only academically but also as compassionate and responsible individuals

Confirmation about teaching...

Allow me to share a pivotal moment in my teaching career that unequivocally affirmed the divine calling bestowed upon me. It was a juncture where the intricacies of education seamlessly intertwined with the spiritual dimensions of discernment.

There was a particular instance when, with what some might call intuition but what I believe is divine discernment, I sensed an impending challenge before it materialized in the physical realm. It was as if God had granted me a foresight, a glimpse into the spiritual undercurrents that often precede tangible events. In this instance, I felt a subtle nudge, an inner knowing that there might be an issue with a parent that could potentially affect the harmony of the classroom. Armed with this spiritual insight, I had the precious gift of time—time to prepare emotionally, mentally, and practically for what lay ahead. This was not just a lucky guess or a fortunate coincidence; it was a confirmation of the divine guidance that accompanies a true calling. It affirmed that teaching is not merely a profession but a sacred journey where God's wisdom becomes a beacon, illuminating the path ahead.

As the events unfolded, I found myself equipped with an innate understanding of the spiritual dynamics at play, allowing me to navigate the upcoming parent issue with grace, empathy, and a sense of divine purpose. This experience crystallized for me the profound connection between teaching and divine guidance.

Moments like these transcend the ordinary challenges of a teacher's life, transcending them into opportunities for spiritual growth and deeper connection with the calling. It's the kind of confirmation that fortifies one's commitment to the teaching profession, reinforcing the belief that, indeed, teaching is not just a career but a divine mission where each step is guided by a higher purpose.

Connecting with the spiritual aspects of your role,

In the tapestry of education, especially in the face of challenges, educators can weave a deeper connection with the spiritual dimensions of their role, transforming their journey into one that is not only effective but profoundly meaningful.

Beyond the textbooks that line our classrooms, educators must anchor their teaching in a belief system that transcends the mundane. Connecting teaching to a higher purpose, to God, elevates the impact of our efforts. It's not just about imparting knowledge; it is about imparting wisdom, compassion, and a sense of divine guidance.

Practical ways to foster this connection include incorporating moments of reflection and prayer into the daily rhythm of the classroom. Taking a few moments at the start or end of the day to center yourself spiritually can provide the strength and resilience needed to navigate challenges. This intentional pause allows educators to invite God into their professional lives, acknowledging that, with this spiritual connection, they embark on a journey where failure is not an option.

Moreover, educators can infuse spiritual principles into their teaching methodologies. For instance, emphasizing values such as kindness, empathy, and gratitude creates a classroom environment that reflects a deeper understanding of our interconnectedness. When educators consciously integrate these principles into their interactions, they not only enrich the learning experience but also create a space where God's presence is palpable.

In challenging times, this spiritual connection becomes a source of unwavering support. Believing that God is intricately woven into the fabric of their profession, educators can find solace in the knowledge that they are not alone. This belief becomes a guiding light, providing strength, resilience, and a sense of purpose that transcends the difficulties at hand.

By consciously connecting with the spiritual aspects of their role, educators transform their classrooms into sacred spaces, where the divine presence infuses every lesson, every interaction, and every challenge with purpose and meaning.

Divine calling influences your approach…

Embracing teaching as a divine calling has not only shaped my philosophy but has become the guiding force behind every facet of my approach to education. This profound perspective echoes through my interactions with students, parents, colleagues, and the broader community, illuminating the transformative power that comes with recognizing teaching as a sacred mission.

In the tapestry of daily challenges, this perspective acts as a compass, guiding us to navigate situations with grace and wisdom. For instance, when faced with difficult conversations or situations, I find myself drawing from a wellspring of patience and compassion that transcends the ordinary. It is the understanding that my role extends beyond the transmission of knowledge—it involves teaching, guiding, leading, protecting, defending, and modeling virtues that extend beyond the academic realm.

There are days when the weight of responsibilities feels overwhelming, and it's in those moments that the divine calling becomes a beacon of strength. Recognizing that others are depending on me to fulfill not just a job but a purpose, a calling, instills a sense of resilience that goes beyond personal challenges. It becomes a reminder that there is a profound significance in what I do, a purpose that extends beyond myself, fueled by a divine energy that sustains and uplifts.

Moreover, this perspective influences the way I engage with colleagues. Instead of viewing them solely as coworkers, I see them as fellow stewards of a sacred mission, each contributing to the collective effort of shaping young minds and hearts. The collaborative spirit takes on a deeper meaning when grounded in the awareness that we are part of something greater than ourselves.

Embracing teaching as a divine calling has infused my professional journey with purpose, resilience, and a heightened sense of responsibility. It's not just a job; it's a sacred trust that requires a constant commitment to excellence, empathy, and the recognition that, in the realm of education, we are instruments of a higher purpose—a purpose that transcends the ordinary and transforms the act of teaching into a sacred and fulfilling calling.

Recognizing the calling impacts culture and environment?

Undoubtedly, recognizing teaching as a calling significantly shapes the very fabric of a school's culture and environment. The impact is profound and multi-faceted, influencing not only student perceptions but also fostering a collective ethos among educators.

When teachers carry themselves with the acknowledgment that they are engaged in a divine calling, it radiates through their attitude, style, and persona. It's more than just a job; it's a sacred duty. This sense of purpose commands a unique respect from students, as they intuitively recognize when a teacher is grounded in something greater than themselves. It's the authority of God woven into the very fabric of the classroom, shaping not just academic lessons but the overall character and atmosphere of the learning environment.

Consider, for instance, a teacher whose love for their vocation is evident in every interaction. This love, stemming from a recognition of teaching as a calling, becomes a contagious force. Students pick up on the positive energy, dedication, and the sense of purpose that permeates the classroom. It's an environment where learning is not just about acquiring information but about personal growth, respect, and a shared journey toward knowledge.

Moreover, the impact extends beyond student-teacher dynamics. When educators collectively recognize teaching as a calling, it creates a culture of collaboration and shared purpose among the staff. There's a mutual understanding that they are not just colleagues; they are co-stewards of a sacred mission. This shared ethos fosters a supportive community where everyone is inspired to bring their best selves into the educational journey.

The recognition of teaching as a calling becomes a transformative force, shaping the school culture into a haven of positivity, respect, and shared purpose. It's a ripple effect, where the teachers' connection to something positive—God's authority in their lives—creates a resonance that permeates every corner of the school environment. Through this recognition, the school becomes not just a place of learning but a sanctuary where the divine presence is felt, and the journey of education becomes a collective, meaningful endeavor.

Religious texts resonate with teaching profession as a divine calling?

Absolutely, the rich tapestry of religious texts and spiritual teachings holds passages that deeply resonate with my conviction that teaching is a divine calling. One such poignant example comes from *The Bible* (Christianity):

Ephesians 4:11-12 (NIV): "So Christ himself gave the apostles, the prophets, the evangelists, the pastors and teachers, to equip his people for works of service, so that the body of Christ may be built up."

2 Timothy 4:2 (NIV): "Preach the word; be prepared in season and out of season; correct, rebuke and encourage—with great patience and careful instruction."

The Quran (Islam):

Surah Al-Baqarah (2:129): "Our Lord, send among them a messenger of their own who will recite to them Your verses and teach them the Book and wisdom and purify them. Indeed, you are the Exalted in Might, the Wise."

The Bhagavad Gita (Hinduism):

Chapter 4, Verse 1: "The Blessed Lord said: I instructed this imperishable science of yoga to the sun-god, Vivasvan, and Vivasvan instructed it to Manu, the father of mankind, and Manu in turn instructed it to Ikshvaku."

The Hadith (Islam):

Sahih Bukhari: "The Prophet (peace be upon him) said: 'The example of guidance and knowledge with which Allah has sent me is like abundant rain falling on the earth, some of which was fertile soil that absorbed rainwater and brought forth vegetation and grass in abundance.'"

In [Ephesians 4:11-12 (NIV)], the essence of teaching as a sacred mission is beautifully encapsulated, serving as a guiding light in my understanding of the profound spiritual dimensions of education.

This passage speaks to the transformative power of imparting knowledge, emphasizing not only the academic facets of teaching but also the moral and spiritual responsibility that comes with it. It underscores the idea that educators are not just disseminators of information, but stewards entrusted with the sacred duty of shaping hearts and minds.

Additionally, [2 Timothy 4:2 (NIV)] reinforces the concept that teaching is not merely a profession but a divine calling. It delves into the idea that the act of teaching is an act of service to a higher purpose, a calling that goes beyond the immediate classroom setting and extends into the spiritual growth of individuals.

Personally, these passages have been a source of inspiration and guidance in my journey as an educator. They serve as reminders that the noble profession of teaching is intricately connected to something greater than us. The wisdom encapsulated in these texts infuses my approach to education with a profound sense of purpose and responsibility.

By drawing upon these timeless teachings, I find strength, solace, and a reaffirmation of the sacred nature of teaching. It's a continual dialogue with the divine through the words of these revered texts, shaping not only my understanding of the profession but also influencing the way I engage with my students and colleagues. In this way, the wisdom contained in religious and spiritual passages becomes a living, breathing part of my teaching philosophy—a philosophy that sees education as a divine calling with the power to transform lives.

Navigating challenges in your profession …

Navigating the challenges in the teaching profession with a sense of divine purpose is a journey that requires intentional and heartfelt practices. Personally, I've found that incorporating God into the very fabric of my day serves as a powerful anchor during turbulent times.

One practical strategy that has been transformative for me is to start each day with a moment of connection with the divine. Before stepping into the classroom, I dedicate time to prayer, seeking guidance, wisdom, and strength from a higher power. This ritual not only centers me but also infuses my actions with a profound sense of purpose. It's as if, with every step, I am walking in alignment with a divine plan.

Moreover, at the conclusion of each day, I make it a point to express gratitude to God. Reflecting on the day's challenges and triumphs, I offer thanks for the opportunities to make a positive impact, for the growth achieved, and for the support received. This practice of gratitude becomes a closing ceremony, a way to acknowledge the divine presence in both the ordinary and extraordinary moments of my professional life.

In the face of challenges, this intentional connection with God serves as a source of insurance—an unwavering assurance that, regardless of the obstacles encountered, there is a divine purpose at play. It provides a perspective that extends beyond the immediate difficulties, reminding me that I am part of a greater narrative shaped by divine wisdom.

For educators facing similar challenges, my advice goes beyond the routine of prayer. It's about fostering a genuine relationship with the divine, where moments of reflection, gratitude, and seeking guidance become integral parts of your teaching practice. Share your challenges with God as you would with a trusted friend and allow that connection to infuse your actions with purpose and resilience.

Remember, it's not just about seeking divine assistance when storms arise; it's about cultivating a continuous dialogue with the divine that permeates every aspect of your professional life. In doing so, you'll find that challenges become opportunities for growth, and the teaching profession transforms into a sacred journey guided by a higher purpose.

Fostering a sense of purpose and calling…

Fostering a sense of purpose and calling among students is a sacred responsibility that teachers carry. It begins with the intentional cultivation of a positive learning environment, and this can be achieved through strategic approaches that extend beyond mere classroom management.

One powerful strategy is to set a tone of inspiration right from the beginning of the learning journey. This involves framing lessons not just as a transfer of information but as a voyage of discovery, a journey that holds personal and collective significance. Consider, for example, incorporating stories of individuals whose lives were transformed through education. By sharing narratives of people who found purpose and calling in their academic pursuits, teachers can instill a sense of possibility and meaning in the minds of their students.

Furthermore, teachers play a crucial role as models for their students. It's not just about what we teach but how we embody the principles of purpose and calling. Demonstrating passion for our subject matter, showcasing genuine curiosity, and conveying the real-world applications of knowledge all contribute to fostering a sense of purpose. When students witness their teachers approaching education not as a task but as a lifelong journey of growth and discovery, it ignites a spark within them to seek a broader significance in their own learning.

Another dimension to consider is the connection between education and the greater community. Teachers can guide students in understanding how their education is not isolated but interconnected with the world around them. This involves incorporating service-learning projects, inviting guest speakers, or organizing field trips that showcase the practical applications of academic knowledge in real-life scenarios.

Importantly, teachers must be vigilant about the tone they set in the classroom. Negativity can quickly extinguish the flame of curiosity and purpose. By fostering an atmosphere of encouragement, constructive feedback, and a belief in each student's potential, teachers provide fertile ground where a sense of purpose can take root and flourish.

The broader significance of education lies not just in the acquisition of knowledge but in the transformation of individuals into lifelong learners who recognize the profound calling embedded in their academic pursuits. As teachers, our role extends beyond curriculum delivery; it encompasses the nurturing of purpose-driven individuals who will, in turn, contribute meaningfully to the world around them.

Addressing resistance or skepticism…

Encountering resistance or skepticism regarding the notion of teaching as a divine calling is not uncommon. It's a perspective that invites a spectrum of beliefs, ranging from those who attribute their actions solely to personal merits to others who find resonance in a broader, divine theory. In navigating these differing viewpoints, I've found that fostering open dialogue is crucial. Instead of viewing skepticism as a roadblock, I see it as an opportunity for meaningful conversations that bridge the gap between diverse perspectives. For instance, when confronted with the notion that everything one does is based on personal merits, I often share personal anecdotes or stories from fellow educators who have experienced moments of transcendence in their teaching journey—moments where the ordinary transforms into the extraordinary.

Moreover, I acknowledge the validity of scientific theories, such as the Big Bang theory, while also highlighting the compatibility of these theories with a spiritual worldview. The divine theory doesn't negate scientific principles; rather, it invites a broader perspective that encompasses both the measurable and the immeasurable aspects of our existence. In this way, teaching as a divine calling becomes a complementary narrative that adds depth and purpose to the everyday actions of educators.

It's important to emphasize that recognizing teaching as a divine calling doesn't diminish the value of personal merits; instead, it elevates the meaning behind those merits. Every skill, every achievement becomes a manifestation of a higher purpose, contributing to the collective tapestry of education.

Addressing skepticism involves not just defending a perspective but inviting others into a journey of exploration. It's about finding common ground and celebrating the richness that diverse beliefs bring to the teaching profession. By fostering understanding and highlighting the harmony between personal merits, scientific theories, and the spiritual dimensions of teaching, we create a more inclusive and enriching dialogue that transcends differences and unites us in our shared commitment to education as a profound and meaningful calling.

Scriptures
That support The Calling

Jeremiah 29:11 (NIV): "For I know the plans I have for you, declares the Lord, plans for welfare and not for evil, to give you a future and a hope."

Proverbs 22:6 (NIV): "Start children off on the way they should go, and even when they are old, they will not turn from it."

Colossians 3:23-24 (NIV): "Whatever you do, work at it with all your heart, as working for the Lord, not for human masters, since you know that you will receive an inheritance from the Lord as a reward. It is the Lord Christ you are serving."

2 Timothy 1:9 (NIV): "He has saved us and called us to a holy life—not because of anything we have done but because of his own purpose and grace."

Ephesians 2:10 (NIV): "For we are God's handiwork, created in Christ Jesus to do good works, which God prepared in advance for us to do."

Matthew 28:19-20 (NIV): "Therefore, go and make disciples of all nations, baptizing them in the name of the Father and of the Son and of the Holy Spirit, and teaching them to obey everything I have commanded you."

1 Corinthians 12:4-7 (NIV): "There are different kinds of gifts, but the same Spirit distributes them. There are different kinds of service, but the same Lord.

There are different kinds of working, but in all of them and in everyone it is the same God at work."

Isaiah 54:13 (NIV): "All your children will be taught by the Lord, and great will be their peace."

Psalm 32:8 (NIV): "I will instruct you and teach you in the way you should go; I will counsel you with my loving eye on you."

Romans 12:6-8 (NIV): "We have different gifts, according to the grace given to each of us. If your gift is prophesying, then prophesy in accordance with your faith; if it is serving, then serve; if it is teaching, then teach."

These scriptures provide a biblical foundation for the idea that teaching is not just a profession but a divine calling, offering encouragement and inspiration for educators to embrace their role with a sense of purpose and faith.

CHAPTER 2:

Navigating Classroom Challenges: Strategies for Effective Classroom Management

Managing classroom dynamics is a multifaceted challenge, and throughout my career, I've encountered various scenarios that demanded nuanced approaches. One prevalent challenge lies in navigating cultural differences, where students' behaviors are often influenced by their religious and cultural backgrounds.

To address this, I've found that building a strong foundation of understanding is paramount. It involves not only acknowledging the cultural diversity present in the classroom but actively seeking to comprehend the nuances that shape students' perspectives. For instance, I vividly recall a situation where cultural differences became evident in the form of communication styles. By taking the time to learn about the diverse communication norms within the class, I was able to adapt my teaching approach to create an inclusive and respectful environment.

Furthermore, I've consistently found value in establishing a connection with students' parents. This extends beyond addressing behavioral concerns; it involves proactively engaging with parents to celebrate their child's successes, both behaviorally and academically. Anecdotes of positive achievements serve as bridges between the classroom and the home, fostering a collaborative partnership that enhances the overall classroom dynamic.

One particularly memorable experience involved a student from a different cultural background who initially seemed disengaged in class. Through regular communication with the student's parents, I discovered a passion for a specific cultural activity. By incorporating this interest into the classroom, not only did the student become more engaged, but it also created an opportunity for cultural exchange among classmates.

In addition to these personal anecdotes, there are several practical strategies that educators can implement to address cultural differences in the classroom. This includes incorporating diverse perspectives into the curriculum, fostering open discussions about cultural norms, and creating an inclusive and accepting classroom culture.

Managing classroom dynamics requires a proactive and adaptive approach, especially when it comes to addressing cultural differences. By understanding, celebrating, and leveraging the diverse backgrounds of students, we not only overcome challenges but create an enriched learning environment where every student feels valued and understood.

Maintaining a positive learning environment despite challenges…

Successfully maintaining a positive learning environment amidst classroom challenges is a dynamic process that requires a combination of practical strategies and, in my belief, divine guidance. One example that stands out involves a situation where a significant number of students in my class were displaying disruptive behavior, hindering the learning experience for everyone.

In tackling this challenge, the first step was seeking support not only from colleagues but also from a higher source. Before the school day commenced and at its conclusion, I made it a practice to engage in prayer. This ritual served as a grounding mechanism, providing me with clarity, patience, and resilience in the face of adversity.

Recognizing that unity among teachers is crucial, I reached out to my colleagues to assess if similar behaviors were manifesting in their classrooms. This collaborative effort helped in identifying patterns and allowed us to collectively strategize on effective interventions. It was not just about addressing isolated incidents but fostering a school-wide approach to behavioral challenges.

Next, I took the initiative to connect with my parents. Maintaining open lines of communication, whether through phone calls or utilizing online platforms, proved instrumental. Rather than simply addressing the misbehavior, these interactions became opportunities to create a partnership with parents. I shared my concerns, sought their insights, and collectively discussed ways to manage their child's behavior for the benefit of their learning experience.

In one particularly challenging instance, where students seemed disinterested and disruptive during instruction, I implemented a targeted approach. After seeking divine guidance through prayer, I made a deliberate effort to connect with each student individually. Understanding their unique perspectives, challenges, and interests allowed me to tailor my approach to meet their needs. This personalized engagement not only improved behavior but also created a more positive and inclusive classroom atmosphere.

The culmination of these strategies, grounded in both practical collaboration and spiritual reflection, yielded positive outcomes. Not only did the disruptive behavior subside, but there was a noticeable shift in the overall classroom dynamic. Students became more engaged, respectful, and invested in the learning process.

This experience reinforced my belief that effective classroom management goes beyond conventional methods; it requires a holistic approach that embraces collaboration, personalized attention, and a connection to something greater. In navigating challenges, the combination of practical strategies and reliance on a higher power can truly transform the learning environment and the lives of the students we are privileged to teach.

Establishing clear expectations…

Establishing clear expectations for behavior in the classroom is not merely a procedural task but a profound opportunity to set the tone for a positive and respectful learning environment. To achieve this, I believe in the power of prayer and divine guidance as foundational elements in shaping the parameters of our classroom community.

From the very first day of class, I begin with a moment of reflection and prayer. This intentional act serves as a collective grounding for both me and the students. It creates a sacred space where we acknowledge the importance of mutual respect, cooperation, and a shared commitment to learning. By infusing the classroom with a sense of divine purpose, students recognize that their behaviors are not only accountable to me but also to something greater than themselves.

In practical terms, these moments of prayer set the stage for a collaborative discussion about expectations. I engage the students in a dialogue where we collectively define what respectful and responsible behavior looks like in our classroom. This collaborative approach not only empowers students to take ownership of their conduct but also fosters a sense of community where everyone's voice is valued.

Moreover, I reinforce these expectations through positive reinforcement and acknowledgment of desirable behaviors. This can take the form of praise, recognition, or small incentives that celebrate individual and collective adherence to the established norms. In doing so, students begin to associate positive behaviors with a sense of accomplishment and recognition.

An illustrative example involves a class agreement co-created with students. This agreement, developed through our initial discussions and revisited periodically, becomes a visual representation of our shared expectations. It hangs prominently in the classroom, serving as a constant reminder of the standards we collectively uphold.

Through these intentional practices, I've witnessed the transformative impact on classroom dynamics. Students enter the learning space with a heightened awareness of the values we hold dear, creating an atmosphere where respect and cooperation are not just expected but celebrated. The spiritual foundation laid through prayer becomes a guiding force that transcends individual behaviors, contributing to the effective management of our classroom and fostering a positive and purposeful educational experience.

Teacher's attitude impact classroom atmosphere?

The teacher's attitude and demeanor are indeed the linchpin of classroom dynamics, functioning as a powerful force that sets the tone for the entire learning environment. Students take cues from the teacher, making them the central figure in the classroom narrative.

In my experience, I've witnessed firsthand the transformative influence that a positive teacher demeanor can have on student behavior and engagement. The teacher serves as the orchestrator of the educational experience, and when that conductor exudes positivity, it creates a harmonious and conducive atmosphere for learning. A key element in fostering this positivity is the connection with God's guidance. Students are intuitive and can sense when there is a deeper, positive influence shaping the classroom dynamics.

Consider an instance where a challenging topic needed to be addressed. Instead of approaching it with apprehension, I consciously chose to frame it as an opportunity for growth and understanding. By maintaining a positive and confident demeanor, I noticed a ripple effect among the students. Their receptiveness increased, and a sense of shared optimism replaced any potential negativity.

The equation of positivity, as I've come to understand, operates like a formula. When the teacher radiates positivity and relates to divine guidance, students respond in kindness. It's a synergistic relationship where the energy invested in cultivating a positive environment is reciprocated by the students.

To offer practical strategies, I recommend that teachers start each day with a moment of reflection, prayer, or affirmation to center themselves. This sets the stage for maintaining a positive attitude throughout the day. Additionally, consciously choosing positive language, expressing enthusiasm for the subject matter, and actively acknowledging students' efforts contribute to a favorable classroom atmosphere.

In challenging moments, framing difficulties as opportunities for growth and learning can shift the overall tone. Moreover, maintaining open communication with students, listening to their perspectives, and offering constructive feedback in a positive manner fosters a respectful and collaborative atmosphere.

The teacher's attitude is a potent catalyst for either positive or negative classroom dynamics. By embracing positivity, connecting with divine guidance, and employing intentional strategies, teachers can create an environment where learning thrives, and students feel inspired to contribute positively to the educational journey.

Communication play in managing classroom ...

Communication stands as the cornerstone in the effective management of classroom challenges, wielding a transformative influence on the outcome of various expectations. The manner in which a teacher communicates becomes the linchpin that either mitigates or exacerbates challenges.

Consider a scenario where a complex assignment is introduced to the class. The clarity of communication in explaining the task, the expectations, and the assessment criteria significantly impacts how well students grasp and execute the assignment. Through precise and transparent communication, potential sources of confusion are preemptively addressed, laying the groundwork for a smoother and more successful learning experience.

Beyond clarity, the tone and approach of communication are equally crucial. I've found that adopting an open and approachable demeanor fosters an environment where students feel comfortable seeking clarification or expressing concerns. This proactive form of communication is a preemptive measure against potential challenges, as it encourages students to engage in a dialogue that can prevent misunderstandings from snowballing into larger issues.

To effectively communicate expectations to students, it's vital to employ a multi-faceted approach. One strategy involves the use of visual aids, such as charts or diagrams, to complement verbal instructions. This not only caters to diverse learning styles but also reinforces the clarity of communicated expectations.

Another impactful technique is the establishment of a class agreement collaboratively with students. By involving them in the process, teachers not only communicate expectations but also instill a sense of ownership among students. This shared agreement serves as a reference point, reminding students of the collective commitment to a positive and respectful classroom environment.

Moreover, periodic check-ins through one-on-one discussions or class reflections provide opportunities to assess how well students are internalizing communicated expectations. It's a dynamic and ongoing process that ensures expectations remain at the forefront of the learning experience.

Effective communication is not just a conduit for information but a dynamic tool that shapes the classroom environment. By prioritizing clarity, approachability, and student involvement, teachers can proactively manage challenges, create a positive atmosphere, and pave the way for a successful and enriching educational journey.

Effective techniques in engaging students and preventing disruptive behavior...

When it comes to engaging students and preventing disruptive behaviors, the effectiveness of techniques largely hinges on an intimate understanding of the unique dynamics within the classroom. It's not a one-size-fits-all scenario; rather, it requires a nuanced approach that considers the individual behaviors and learning styles of the students.

Let's delve into a practical example. If there are students in the class who are naturally exuberant and inclined to express themselves loudly, opting for collaborative learning activities might seem counterintuitive for noise control. In such cases, I've found that taking the activity outdoors during warmer weather can be a game-changer. The change in environment not only caters to the energetic nature of certain students but also allows for a more dynamic and controlled setting.

On the other hand, if independent work is the chosen activity, its effectiveness is heightened when students are genuinely excited about the task at hand. This is where the teacher's role as a facilitator becomes crucial. By tapping into the interests and passions of the students, lessons can be crafted to align with their preferences. For instance, if a class collectively shows enthusiasm for a specific topic, incorporating that theme into the lesson can enhance engagement and contribute to a more focused and positive atmosphere.

A valuable strategy that I've employed is the use of interest inventories. By systematically gauging the learning styles, preferences, and interests of students, teachers gain valuable insights that inform lesson planning. This initiative-taking approach allows for the tailoring of activities to resonate with the diverse ways in which students absorb and engage with information.

For instance, if a significant portion of the class thrives in visual learning, integrating multimedia elements or visual aids can elevate the effectiveness of the lesson. Similarly, if firsthand activities resonate with a particular group, incorporating interactive components can foster a more immersive and engaging learning experience.

The key lies in adaptability and a personalized approach. By leveraging a combination of environmental adjustments, student interests, and insights from interest inventories, teachers can navigate the complexities of classroom dynamics with greater efficacy. The goal is not just to manage behavior but to create an environment where students are inherently drawn to the learning process, resulting in a more meaningful and enriching educational experience.

Addressing individual student needs and differences

Addressing individual student needs and fostering an inclusive classroom environment is a dynamic process that requires a vigilant and intentional approach. One guiding principle I consistently emphasize is the recognition that challenges can arise, and we, as stewards, must be equipped with our full armor to navigate them successfully.

To bring this concept into practicality, consider a situation where a student faces specific learning challenges. Instead of viewing it solely as an obstacle, I approach it as an opportunity to tailor my teaching methods. For instance, incorporating varied instructional approaches, such as visual aids, interactive activities, or providing additional support, ensures that individual needs are met.

Moreover, the metaphor of putting on the full armor extends beyond the classroom, encompassing interactions with colleagues, parents, and administrators. Open and transparent communication is a critical component. Engaging in regular conversations with parents about their child's unique strengths and areas of growth establishes a collaborative partnership in supporting the student's holistic development.

In terms of classroom dynamics, a key strategy is fostering a sense of unity and understanding among students. I actively encourage an atmosphere where differences are celebrated rather than stigmatized. This can be achieved through inclusive activities that highlight the diversity of perspectives and experiences within the class.

For example, incorporating literature, history, or cultural elements that resonate with the varied backgrounds of students not only makes the curriculum more relatable but also instills a sense of pride and belonging. Furthermore, implementing cooperative learning structures promotes peer support, allowing students to learn from each other's strengths and differences.

The notion of putting on full armor becomes a guiding principle in navigating the multifaceted landscape of individual student needs and differences. By embracing an initiative-taking and inclusive mindset, we not only address challenges but create an environment where every student feels seen, valued, and equipped to thrive in their unique educational journey.

Advice on handling conflicts or disruptions in the classroom

Handling conflicts or disruptions in the classroom requires a nuanced approach that considers the individual dynamics of each learning environment. While what works for one may not work for another, there are overarching principles that I've found universally applicable in maintaining a focus on student learning amidst challenges.

Firstly, the belief in being called by God brings a sense of assurance and purpose to the teaching profession. When conflicts arise, I've often turned to prayer for guidance and understanding. Seeking divine wisdom allows for a perspective that goes beyond immediate challenges, fostering a mindset focused on the holistic well-being and learning of each student.

Practical advice for handling conflicts involves maintaining a calm and composed demeanor. During disruptions, it's crucial to convey a sense of control and assurance. Addressing conflicts privately and with empathy allows for a more constructive resolution, preserving the dignity of the student involved.

Furthermore, the classroom environment should be one where open communication is encouraged. Establishing a culture where students feel safe to express their concerns or frustrations fosters a proactive approach to conflict resolution. Through respectful dialogue, conflicts can be transformed into opportunities for growth and understanding.

In instances where beliefs about being called by God may differ, a shared commitment to the well-being and learning of students serves as common ground. Emphasizing the overarching purpose of education—to nurture and guide the next generation—can create a collaborative mindset, even among those with different philosophical perspectives.

Ultimately, the key is to approach conflicts with a combination of faith, empathy, and practical strategies. By seeking guidance from a higher source, maintaining composure, fostering open communication, and emphasizing the shared goal of student development, teachers can navigate challenges with resilience and contribute to a positive and focused learning environment.

Strategies for building positive relationships with students...

The process of building positive relationships with students is akin to solving a mathematical equation, where each element contributes to the overall solution. To truly understand and connect with students, it's essential to read the entire 'equation' by delving into their individual likes and dislikes.

One fundamental strategy is proactive inquiry into students' preferences, interests, and personal experiences. This goes beyond the formalities of the classroom and involves taking a genuine interest in each student's unique identity. By asking about their hobbies, favorite subjects, or even their weekend adventures, teachers can uncover valuable insights that serve as the foundation for meaningful connections.

An additional strategy involves creating a classroom culture that fosters open communication. Establishing an environment where students feel comfortable expressing their thoughts and concerns builds trust. This open dialogue extends beyond academic matters and delves into the personal aspects of students' lives, further strengthening the teacher-student relationship.

Furthermore, incorporating personalized elements into the learning experience contributes to relationship-building. For example, acknowledging birthdays, achievements, or even challenges that students may be facing demonstrates empathy and reinforces the teacher's commitment to the holistic well-being of each student.

The benefits of these positive relationships extend to effective classroom management. When students feel seen, heard, and understood, there is a natural inclination to reciprocate that respect. This mutual understanding creates a harmonious atmosphere where students are more likely to be engaged, cooperative, and responsive to the teacher's guidance.

The equation for building positive relationships involves a combination of genuine inquiry, open communication, and personalized engagement. The dividends paid in terms of effective classroom management are immense, as a connected and engaged student body forms the bedrock of a conducive learning environment.

Involving students in creating a positive classroom culture,

Teachers bear the responsibility of not only fostering positive connections with students but also empowering them to actively contribute to the creation of a positive classroom culture. It's not just about attracting positive behavior; it's about cultivating an environment where students feel a sense of ownership and agency in shaping their learning experience.

One impactful strategy involves soliciting students' input on classroom norms and expectations. Rather than imposing rules, collaborative discussions allow students to voice their perspectives and collectively establish a set of guidelines. This inclusive approach not only communicates a sense of respect for their opinions but also instills a shared commitment to a positive learning environment.

Additionally, incorporating student-led initiatives or projects contributes to a sense of ownership. Whether it's a class project, a bulletin board showcasing students' achievements, or involvement in decision-making processes, these opportunities foster a genuine investment in the classroom culture. Students become active participants rather than passive recipients, leading to increased engagement and a more positive atmosphere.

For instance, implementing a student council or a classroom leadership team provides a platform for students to play a direct role in decision-making. This not only empowers them but also enhances their sense of responsibility for the well-being of the class.

The impact of student involvement extends beyond the immediate classroom setting to influence behavior and engagement school wide. As students take pride in their contributions to a positive culture, there's a ripple effect that permeates the broader school community. Positive behavior becomes a collective norm, and engagement is heightened as students recognize the direct impact of their actions on the overall learning environment.

Involving students in shaping the classroom culture goes beyond attracting positive behavior; it cultivates a sense of ownership and responsibility. This not only enhances engagement within the classroom but also contributes to a positive school-wide culture where students actively contribute to the collective success of the learning community.

These questions aim to extract practical tips, personal experiences, and actionable advice from Dr. Dayse, offering readers valuable insights into effective classroom management strategies.

Scriptures That support Navigating the Classroom Challenges

Proverbs 15:1 (NIV): "A gentle answer turns away wrath, but a harsh word stirs up anger."

Philippians 4:6-7 (NIV): "Do not be anxious about anything, but in every situation, by prayer and petition, with thanksgiving, present your requests to God. And the peace of God, which transcends all understanding, will guard your hearts and your minds in Christ Jesus."

James 1:19 (NIV): "My dear brothers and sisters, take note of this: Everyone should be quick to listen, slow to speak and slow to become angry."

Colossians 3:23 (NIV): "Whatever you do, work at it with all your heart, as working for the Lord, not for human masters."

Proverbs 22:6 (NIV): "Start children off on the way they should go, and even when they are old, they will not turn from it."

Ephesians 4:32 (NIV): "Be kind and compassionate to one another, forgiving each other, just as in Christ God forgave you."

Proverbs 3:5-6 (NIV): "Trust in the Lord with all your heart and lean not on your own understanding; in all your ways submit to him, and he will make your paths straight."

1 Corinthians 14:40 (NIV): "But everything should be done in a fitting and orderly way."

Psalm 119:165 (NIV): "Great peace have those who love your law, and nothing can make them stumble."

Matthew 5:9 (NIV): "Blessed are the peacemakers, for they will be called children of God."

CHAPTER 3:

Dealing with Difficult Parents: Finding Grace and Patience

Common challenges teachers face

Teachers often encounter challenges when dealing with difficult parents, particularly those who may not share the same values or beliefs. One common obstacle is the expectation for teachers to perform miracles in their child's education, as if learning were a supernatural act. Navigating such challenges requires a delicate balance of grace, patience, and effective communication.

In my own experiences, I've found that acknowledging the limitations of education and emphasizing the collaborative nature of the teacher-parent-student relationship is crucial. By gently conveying that education is a partnership and that success is a collective effort, it becomes easier to manage unrealistic expectations.

Moreover, when faced with parents who may not know the Lord or lack patience and respect for truth, it becomes an opportunity to exemplify the virtues of James 1:19-20. Adopting a posture of being quick to listen, slow to speak, and slow to become angry fosters an environment conducive to understanding and resolution. Rather than reacting defensively, I strive to engage in open dialogue, seeking to understand the concerns and perspectives of the parents.

One effective strategy is to highlight positive aspects of the child's behavior or achievements. By focusing on shared goals and positive attributes, it becomes possible to build common ground even with parents who may not be familiar with biblical teachings. This approach helps shift the conversation from adversarial to collaborative, fostering a more constructive relationship. Additionally, providing resources and suggestions for parents on how to support their child's behavioral and academic development at home can be beneficial. This not only empowers parents but also demonstrates the teacher's commitment to the overall well-being and success of the student.

Navigating challenges with difficult parents involves a combination of empathy, effective communication, and a focus on shared goals. By fostering understanding and collaboration, teachers can bridge the gap with parents, even when faced with differing beliefs or expectations.

Instances where issues were resolved with parents through communication

One poignant instance that stands out involves a situation where one student had physically harmed another. In navigating this delicate issue, I drew upon the teachings of patience, stillness, and the biblical directive not to worry but to pray about everything.

Before addressing the parents, I made a conscious effort to seek guidance from a higher source. By incorporating prayer into my daily routine—both before school and after—I found a sense of peace and assurance that transcended the challenges at hand. This spiritual foundation offered me a level of protection that surpassed the support of any teacher's union.

Approaching the parent, I prioritized open communication and empathy. Rather than placing blame, I sought to understand the root causes of the behavior and collaborated with the parent on a solution. I shared my commitment to the well-being and success of their child and emphasized the importance of working together as a team.

During the conversation, I actively listened to the concerns of the parents, validating their perspective while gently offering insights from my observations in the classroom. The goal was not only to resolve the immediate issue but to establish a foundation for ongoing communication and collaboration.

The impact of this approach was twofold. Firstly, it resulted in a resolution to the specific incident, fostering a sense of understanding and cooperation between the parent, the student, and myself. Secondly, it laid the groundwork for a positive and constructive relationship with the parent, contributing to a more supportive and engaged partnership throughout the academic journey of their child.

The combination of prayer, trust in the Lord, and a commitment to open and empathetic communication proved to be transformative in navigating this challenging parent-teacher interaction. It reinforced the idea that, beyond the practical strategies, the infusion of spiritual principles can significantly enhance the effectiveness of conflict resolution and relationship-building in the realm of education.

Establishing and maintaining open lines of communication

Establishing and maintaining open lines of communication with parents is a cornerstone of successful teaching. From the very first day of the school year, I prioritize consistent and transparent communication to build rapport and trust. However, recognizing that challenges are inevitable, I've implemented strategies to address concerns and maintain a positive relationship.

One effective approach is the use of multiple communication channels. Utilizing a combination of traditional methods, such as newsletters or handouts, and modern platforms, such as emails, class websites, or communication apps, ensures that information reaches parents through channels most convenient for them. This approach acknowledges the diverse ways in which parents prefer to receive updates and fosters a more inclusive environment.

Moreover, I proactively initiate communication, not only when issues arise but as a regular practice. Providing regular updates on students' progress, achievements, and classroom activities establishes an ongoing dialogue. This approach helps create a positive atmosphere, making it more likely that parents will feel comfortable reaching out to their own concerns.

When addressing concerns or issues, I prioritize empathy and active listening. Rather than solely conveying information, I seek to understand the parent's perspective, acknowledging their concerns and collaboratively exploring potential solutions. This two-way communication fosters a sense of partnership, where both teacher and parent are invested in the success and well-being of the student.

In essence, the key to establishing and maintaining open lines of communication is a proactive and multi-channel approach that prioritizes transparency, regular updates, and a collaborative mindset. By building a foundation of trust and openness, the teacher-parent relationship becomes a valuable asset in navigating challenges and fostering a supportive learning environment.

Strategies for approaching parent-teacher conferences

One of the most impactful strategies I recommend for approaching parent-teacher conferences, especially with parents who may be challenging to communicate with, is to prioritize building strong connections both with the students and their parents from the outset.

Knowing the children, you teach on a personal level and understanding the dynamics of their families can significantly enhance the effectiveness of these conferences. By establishing a familiar and open line of communication throughout the school year, parents are more likely to be on board during conferences because they are already acquainted with the teacher's style, expectations, and genuine commitment to their child's education.

Concrete steps involve regular communication, not just when issues arise. Providing updates on students' progress, celebrating achievements, and sharing insights into their daily activities fosters a sense of partnership between teachers and parents. This proactive approach lays the groundwork for positive and constructive discussions during conferences.

During the conferences themselves, creating a welcoming and inclusive environment is key. Acknowledging the strengths and achievements of each student before delving into areas of improvement sets a positive tone. Encouraging parents to share their perspectives and concerns demonstrates a willingness to collaborate in the best interest of the child.

Moreover, utilizing technology can enhance the accessibility of information for parents. Offering digital platforms where parents can access real-time updates on their child's academic performance, behavior, and overall well-being further strengthens the connection between home and school.

The recommended strategies revolve around proactive and continuous communication, understanding the unique qualities of each student, and creating an inclusive atmosphere during parent-teacher conferences. By prioritizing these elements, teachers can navigate challenging parent-teacher interactions with grace and foster a supportive partnership for the benefit of the student's educational journey.

How listening contributes to resolving conflicts/ building relationships with parents

In my extensive experience, the practice of active listening has proven to be a cornerstone in resolving conflicts and building positive relationships with parents. It goes beyond merely hearing words; it involves a profound understanding of the emotions, concerns, and perspectives that each person brings to the conversation.

One memorable instance involved a conflict with a parent regarding their child's academic progress. Through active listening, I intentionally focused on understanding not just the surface-level concerns but delving into the underlying emotions and motivations. By doing so, I communicated a genuine commitment to comprehending the parent's perspective.

Practical steps I take to ensure effective active listening include maintaining eye contact, providing verbal affirmations to show that I am engaged, and summarizing key points to demonstrate understanding. These actions create an atmosphere of mutual respect and reinforce the idea that both parties have a valuable contribution to the conversation.

Moreover, my faith has been a guiding force in enhancing my ability to be patient and compassionate during active listening. Trusting in the Lord's wisdom and guidance allows me to approach conflicts with a sense of grace, understanding that the resolution is a collaborative effort.

In the broader context, active listening becomes not just a communication tool but a pathway to building trust and empathy. It transforms conflicts into opportunities for understanding and strengthens the foundation of positive relationships with parents.

The power of active listening lies in its ability to transcend spoken words and tap into the deeper emotions and perspectives of all parties involved. By integrating this practice into parent-teacher interactions, conflicts become steppingstones to stronger, more positive relationships.

Communication techniques or tools that are effective

There are indeed several communication techniques that I find particularly effective in addressing concerns and maintaining a constructive dialogue with parents. One fundamental practice, which has consistently proven transformative in my experiences, is to begin by seeking guidance through prayer before engaging in any communication.

Praying before communicating sets a tone of humility, patience, and a genuine desire for positive outcomes. It allows me to center myself, tap into a source of wisdom beyond my own, and approach the conversation with a mindset focused on understanding and resolution.

Beyond prayer, another effective technique involves active listening. Actively engaging with parents, listening attentively to their concerns, and responding thoughtfully create an environment of mutual respect. It demonstrates a commitment to understanding their perspective and working collaboratively to address the issue at hand.

Additionally, employing clear and empathetic language is crucial. Articulating information in a way that is easily understood, free from jargon, and infused with empathy enhances the effectiveness of communication. This approach fosters a sense of partnership, reassuring parents that their concerns are heard and valued.

In more practical terms, utilizing various communication channels is essential. Providing updates through newsletters, emails, or digital platforms ensures that information reaches parents in a way that aligns with their preferences. This multi-channel approach enhances accessibility and inclusivity in communication.

Lastly, establishing a regular cadence of communication, not just when issues arise, contributes to an ongoing positive relationship. Regular updates on students' progress and achievements demonstrate a commitment to transparency and collaboration.

The combination of prayer, active listening, clear language, and diverse communication channels forms a comprehensive toolkit for addressing concerns and maintaining constructive dialogue with parents. It is through these intentional and thoughtful practices that effective communication becomes a catalyst for understanding, resolution, and the nurturing of positive relationships.

Balancing empathy and understanding when dealing with challenging parents

Balancing empathy and understanding while maintaining professional boundaries is indeed a delicate task, especially in challenging parent interactions. One powerful realization that has guided me through such situations is the recognition that, much like us, challenging parents are individuals who deeply care about their children.

In instances where a parent interaction becomes particularly challenging, I rely on the virtue of patience, understanding that it is crucial not only for the sake of maintaining professional boundaries but also for fostering a positive and constructive dialogue. Patience allows me to approach the situation with a calm demeanor and a willingness to understand the parent's concerns.

One strategy I find effective is to actively listen to the parent's perspective without immediately responding. This not only demonstrates respect for their viewpoint but also provides me with valuable insights into their concerns and motivations. It creates a space for empathy to flourish without compromising the professionalism required in our role as educators.

Setting clear expectations and boundaries from the beginning of the interaction is another key component. Communicating respectfully but firmly ensures that both parties understand the parameters of the conversation. This clarity contributes to a more structured and constructive dialogue, even in challenging circumstances.

Moreover, I make a conscious effort to shift the focus from challenging behavior to underlying concerns. By acknowledging and addressing the root issues, I create an environment where empathy can thrive without sacrificing the professionalism necessary for effective communication.

The art of balancing empathy and maintaining professional boundaries lies in the intentional cultivation of patience, active listening, and clear communication. By incorporating these elements into challenging parent interactions, we can navigate difficulties with grace and foster a collaborative atmosphere centered on the well-being of the child.

Turning negatives into opportunities for collaboration and understanding

The advice I offer on turning negative interactions with parents into opportunities for collaboration and understanding goes hand in hand with a practice that has consistently proven transformative in my experiences—prayer. While it may seem repetitive, the power of prayer is not just a spiritual belief but a practical tool for fostering understanding and collaboration.

Prayer serves as a foundational step, creating a mindset of humility, openness, and a genuine desire for positive outcomes. However, it's crucial to complement this spiritual practice with practical communication strategies to navigate the complexities of parent-teacher interactions.

One effective approach involves initiating a constructive and empathetic conversation. By actively listening to the parent's concerns, acknowledging their perspective, and expressing a genuine commitment to finding common ground, we set the stage for collaborative problem-solving. This approach goes beyond prayer to actively engage in the resolution process.

Moreover, framing the interaction as an opportunity for mutual understanding can shift the narrative. Emphasizing shared goals for the child's well-being and academic success establishes a collaborative tone. It's essential to convey that both the teacher and the parent are partners in the educational journey.

Sharing specific examples or anecdotes can illustrate the transformative power of collaborative efforts alongside prayer. For instance, recounting instances where prayer, coupled with effective communication, led to a positive resolution can inspire confidence in the potential for collaboration.

While prayer serves as a powerful foundation, the active application of communication strategies, empathy, and a collaborative mindset is equally crucial. By combining these elements, we can transform potentially negative interactions into opportunities for understanding, collaboration, and, ultimately, positive outcomes for the child.

Written communication and documentation play a role in managing interactions

Written communication and documentation serve as invaluable tools in managing interactions with difficult parents, playing a pivotal role in fostering clarity, accountability, and effective resolution. While our communication with God may not be documented in the same way, interactions with parents benefit significantly from a systematic approach to documentation.

Consider a scenario where a challenging situation arises with a parent. By promptly and accurately documenting the details of the conversation, including key points, concerns raised, and agreed-upon action steps, we create a tangible record that serves as a reference point. This documentation not only ensures that important information is retained but also provides a structured framework for future interactions.

Practical tips for effective documentation include maintaining a log or record of all significant parent interactions, whether they occur through emails, phone calls, or in-person meetings. In instances where face-to-face communication is involved, sending a follow-up email summarizing the key discussion points reinforces the shared understanding and provides a written record.

Moreover, written communication can extend to proactive measures such as regular newsletters or updates. These documents can serve as a platform for sharing positive achievements, upcoming events, and important information. By fostering a culture of consistent communication, we create an environment where potential conflicts are addressed within a broader context of positive engagement.

While our connection with the divine may not require documentation, the complexities of human interactions, especially with challenging parents, benefit immensely from a well-maintained record. By adopting a systematic approach to documentation, teachers enhance their ability to manage difficult situations effectively and establish a foundation for transparent and accountable communication.

Involving parents in the educational process/ foster a positive partnerships

Involving parents in the educational process is not just a strategy; it's a foundational principle that fosters positive partnerships between home and school. This approach becomes particularly crucial in challenging situations, where the collaboration between teachers and parents can make a significant difference.

One effective strategy I employ is to establish open lines of communication from the very beginning of the school year. Regular updates, newsletters, and invitations to school events create a sense of inclusion and keep parents informed about their child's educational journey. This proactive approach sets the stage for a positive partnership, even before challenging situations arise.

In challenging moments, maintaining parental involvement becomes a beacon of support. For instance, during parent-teacher conferences or meetings, I actively seek parents' perspectives and insights. This not only demonstrates a genuine interest in their input but also allows me to understand their concerns and expectations more fully.

Another powerful strategy is to involve parents in problem-solving processes. When faced with a challenging situation, I invite parents to collaborate on finding solutions. This approach transforms the dynamic from a potential conflict to a shared effort in the best interest of the child. It's amazing how the collective wisdom of teachers and parents, infused with a sense of partnership, can lead to positive resolutions.

Highlighting the benefits of parental involvement is crucial. Beyond the academic progress of the child, it contributes to a positive school culture, strengthens the sense of community, and fosters a shared commitment to the well-being and success of each student.

Involving parents in the educational process is not just a key to keeping fires at bay; it's the foundation of a thriving partnership between home and school. By actively engaging parents, especially in challenging situations, we create a supportive network that significantly enhances the overall educational experience for the child.

Scriptures That support Dealing with Difficult Parents

Ephesians 4:2 (NIV): "Be completely humble and gentle; be patient, bearing with one another in love."

Proverbs 15:18 (NIV): "A hot-tempered person stirs up conflict, but the one who is patient calms a quarrel."

Colossians 3:13 (NIV): "Bear with each other and forgive one another if any of you has a grievance against someone. Forgive as the Lord forgave you."

James 1:19-20 (NIV): "My dear brothers and sisters, take note of this: Everyone should be quick to listen, slow to speak and slow to become angry, because human anger does not produce the righteousness that God desires."

Proverbs 25:15 (NIV): "Through patience a ruler can be persuaded, and a gentle tongue can break a bone."

1 Corinthians 13:4 (NIV): "Love is patient, love is kind. It does not envy, it does not boast, it is not proud."

Philippians 2:3 (NIV): "Do nothing out of selfish ambition or vain conceit. Rather, in humility value others above yourselves."

Matthew 6:14-15 (NIV): "For if you forgive other people when they sin against you, your heavenly Father will also forgive you. But if you do not forgive others their sins, your father will not forgive your sins."

Galatians 5:22-23 (NIV): "But the fruit of the Spirit is love, joy, peace, forbearance, kindness, goodness, faithfulness, gentleness and self-control."

Romans 12:18 (NIV): "If it is possible, as far as it depends on you, live at peace with everyone."

CHAPTER 4:

Colleague Connections: Building Supportive Professional Relationships

Importance of collaboration and teamwork among educators

Collaboration and teamwork among educators are the backbone of a successful and fulfilling educational journey. Drawing parallels to the body of Christ, where each part contributes to a unified purpose, teamwork in education unites us in the shared mission of nurturing and guiding our students toward success.

In my own professional experiences, I've witnessed the transformative power of collaboration. For instance, during a challenging period when we were implementing a new curriculum, the collective effort of the teaching team ensured that we were all on the same page. Each educator brought their unique strengths and insights to the table, creating a dynamic and supportive environment where we could overcome obstacles and adapt to the changing landscape of education.

One memorable example was a collaborative project where teachers from different subjects integrated their lesson plans to create a holistic learning experience. This cross-disciplinary collaboration not only enriched the educational journey for students but also fostered a sense of unity and shared purpose among the educators involved.

Moreover, the teamwork extended beyond the classroom. During times of professional development or when faced with complex challenges, the collaboration among educators became a source of inspiration and shared wisdom. We learned from each other's experiences, celebrated successes together, and navigated obstacles more effectively as a united front.

Collaboration and teamwork amplify the impact of our individual efforts, creating a synergy that goes beyond what any one educator could achieve alone. It is the shared commitment to our calling in education that transforms challenges into opportunities and sets the stage for a more fulfilling and successful educational experience for both educators and students alike.

Can you share examples of successful collaborative projects or initiatives you've been involved in and the positive outcomes they produced? The best examples I can give where is always collaboration is on school committees, IEP meetings and church meetings. All these meetings have one goal in mind: helping children, the environment, or others.

Fostering a culture of collaboration within a school

Throughout my 31-year career, I've had the privilege of participating in various collaborative projects and initiatives that underscore the transformative power of teamwork. One notable example is our involvement in school committees, where educators come together with a shared goal: enhancing the educational experience for our students.

In one specific committee focused on curriculum development, teachers from diverse subjects collaborated to revamp our approach. By pooling our expertise and perspectives, we created a more integrated and engaging curriculum that catered to the diverse learning styles of our students. The positive outcome was reflected in improved student engagement, performance, and an overall sense of enthusiasm in the learning environment.

Another impactful collaborative setting is the Individualized Education Program (IEP) meetings. These gatherings bring together educators, specialists, and parents to tailor educational strategies for students with unique needs. I've witnessed the power of collaboration in crafting personalized plans that address the individual strengths and challenges of each student. The positive outcomes include increased student progress, a sense of inclusivity, and strengthened partnerships with parents.

Outside the school setting, collaboration extends to my involvement in church meetings. While the context differs, the essence remains the same: a group of individuals working together towards a common purpose. In church initiatives, whether focused on community outreach or youth development, the collaborative spirit fosters a sense of unity and shared commitment to making a positive impact.

In each of these collaborative endeavors, positive outcomes are evident not only in the tangible results achieved but also in the strengthened bonds among colleagues, parents, and community members. It reinforces the belief that when we unite with a shared purpose, the possibilities for positive change become limitless.

This revised response provides specific examples and emphasizes the positive outcomes, making the statement more robust and engaging.

Challenges that arise among colleagues, and how to overcome these challenges

"In my extensive experience, I've encountered various challenges in professional relationships among colleagues, and navigating these challenges has been a crucial aspect of building a supportive and effective collaborative environment. One recurring challenge is the presence of disagreements, which, if not handled properly, can hinder the progress of collaborative projects.

In one instance, our committee faced differing opinions on the best approach to implementing a new teaching strategy. Instead of allowing the disagreement to escalate, we initiated open and respectful dialogue. By actively listening to each other's perspectives and finding common ground, we were able to reach a consensus that incorporated the strengths of each suggestion. This experience taught me the importance of fostering a culture of open communication and mutual respect within collaborative teams.

Another challenge is the reluctance of some colleagues to be open and receptive to new ideas or perspectives. To address this, I have found that creating a space for mindfulness and reflection can be transformative. Encouraging colleagues to approach discussions with an open mind, free from preconceived notions, allows for the exploration of innovative solutions and promotes a more positive and inclusive working environment.

In addition, I firmly believe in the significance of including God in the direction of our collaborative efforts. Praying together as a team before embarking on a project has proven to be a powerful practice. It not only aligns our intentions but also fosters a sense of unity and shared purpose, reminding us that our work is guided by a higher calling.

Moreover, maintaining clarity and specificity in our goals and objectives is paramount. Ambiguity can lead to confusion and misunderstandings. I recall a project where our committee set clear, well-defined goals with input from all members. This clarity provided a roadmap for our collective efforts, ensuring that everyone understood the direction and purpose of our collaboration.

Addressing challenges in professional relationships requires a combination of open communication, mindfulness, spiritual guidance, and clarity of purpose. By actively fostering these elements, we can transform challenges into opportunities for growth, collaboration, and ultimately, success.

Role of effective communication in building
relationships, in a team setting

Effective communication is the cornerstone of building supportive professional relationships among educators, and it plays a pivotal role in the success of collaborative efforts. The significance of communication goes beyond simply understanding the committee's objective; it encompasses a multifaceted approach that fosters a culture of teamwork and shared understanding.

One key aspect of enhancing communication skills in a team setting is ensuring clarity of objectives. When everyone on the team has a clear understanding of the committee's goals and purpose, disagreements are less likely to create insurmountable obstacles. This shared clarity becomes the foundation upon which constructive discussions can take place.

Moreover, effective communication involves active listening—an often overlooked yet crucial skill. Educators should prioritize listening to their colleagues, valuing diverse perspectives, and understanding that every voice contributes to the collective wisdom of the team. This not only enriches the collaborative process but also strengthens professional relationships.

Empathy is another essential component of effective communication. Recognizing and understanding the perspectives, challenges, and strengths of colleagues cultivates a supportive environment. By empathizing with the experiences of team members, educators can build rapport and enhance the overall dynamics of the team.

Adaptability in communication styles is also key in a team setting. Different team members may have distinct communication preferences, and educators should be adept at adjusting their approach to accommodate these differences. Flexibility in communication ensures that everyone feels heard and valued, fostering a sense of inclusivity and collaboration.

To further enhance communication skills, educators can engage in professional development opportunities that focus on effective communication strategies. Workshops, training sessions, and collaborative activities can provide valuable insights and practical tools for improving interpersonal communication within a team.

Effective communication in a team setting involves more than just understanding objectives—it requires active listening, empathy, adaptability, and ongoing professional development. By embracing these elements, educators can contribute to a positive and collaborative professional environment that nurtures supportive relationships and enhances the overall effectiveness of their collaborative efforts.

Handling disagreements or conflicts with colleagues

The best way to navigate conflicts with colleagues is to approach the situation with a commitment to understanding, resolution, and, most importantly, prayer. Seeking guidance from God before addressing conflicts not only centers our intentions but also opens our hearts to empathy and compassion.

In handling disagreements, applying conflict resolution strategies becomes essential. One effective method is to create a conducive space for open dialogue. Actively listening to each other's perspectives, concerns, and feelings fosters mutual understanding. However, recognizing that certain conflicts may require additional support, it is perfectly acceptable to involve a mediator. This neutral third party can facilitate communication, ensure both parties are heard, and guide the conversation toward a resolution.

An essential aspect of conflict resolution is acknowledging that miscommunication or misunderstandings may be at the root of conflicts. Taking the time to clarify expectations, roles, or responsibilities can prevent future disagreements. By addressing these potential sources of conflict proactively, we contribute to a more transparent and cooperative working environment.

It's crucial to recognize that conflicts are not solely interpersonal but can also be influenced by external factors. Acknowledging the presence of external challenges and focusing on collaborative problem-solving helps create a workplace culture where colleagues support each other through difficulties.

In the grander scheme, promoting a positive and productive working environment isn't just about conflict resolution; it's about fostering a culture of respect, empathy, and shared goals. A harmonious workplace benefits not only individual well-being but also enhances overall productivity and the collective success of the team.

Building relationships verses different teaching styles or philosophies

Approaching the task of building relationships with colleagues who have different teaching styles or philosophies requires a foundation of internal peace and a genuine appreciation for the diversity of perspectives within the educational community. It's not just about tolerance; it's about recognizing the value that different teaching styles bring to the table.

One effective strategy I employ is to initiate open and respectful conversations. Actively seeking to understand the rationale behind a colleague's teaching style or philosophy creates a space for mutual appreciation. By expressing curiosity and acknowledging the strengths in diverse approaches, we can bridge the gap between differences and find common ground.

In instances where differences in teaching styles may lead to potential conflicts, I often suggest collaborative projects. By working together on shared goals or projects, colleagues can gain insights into each other's methods and discover the synergies that arise when combining diverse approaches.

This collaborative effort not only enhances the professional relationship but also contributes to a richer and more dynamic educational environment.

Moreover, fostering a culture of continuous learning is crucial. Encouraging colleagues to share their experiences, attend workshops together, or engage in peer observations creates opportunities for mutual growth. Recognizing that diversity in teaching styles enriches the educational landscape, I emphasize the collective strength that emerges when we bring together a variety of perspectives.

Building relationships with colleagues who have different teaching styles is not just a matter of coexistence; it's an opportunity for collaboration, learning, and collective growth. Embracing the richness that diverse philosophies bring to the profession contributes to a more vibrant and resilient educational community.

Strategies or activities recommended for team building

In fostering team building among educators, especially in diverse and dynamic educational environments, it's crucial to approach the process with intentionality and a spirit of inclusivity. Over the years, I've discovered specific strategies that have proven effective in creating a cohesive and supportive professional community. However, it's essential to recognize that the effectiveness of these strategies can vary based on the unique characteristics of the team and the educational environment.

One successful approach involves collaborative professional development sessions. These sessions provide a platform for educators to share their expertise, experiences, and innovative teaching methods. Creating a space where colleagues can learn from each other fosters a sense of mutual respect and appreciation for the diverse talents within the team.

Another impactful strategy is team-building activities that extend beyond the professional setting. Organizing social events, such as team lunches, community service projects, or even team-building retreats, offers educators an opportunity to connect on a personal level. Building relationships beyond the confines of the classroom enhances the sense of camaraderie and shared purpose.

Incorporating reflective practices into team meetings is another valuable strategy. Providing time for educators to share their successes, challenges, and lessons learned creates a supportive environment for growth and collaboration. This reflective process allows team members to draw inspiration from each other's experiences.

However, it's important to approach team-building strategies with sensitivity to individual perspectives and potential misconceptions. Communicating openly about the purpose and goals of these activities ensures that everyone feels included and understands the collective benefits of fostering a strong professional community.

Effective team building is a dynamic process that requires thoughtful consideration of the team's unique characteristics. By aligning strategies with the specific needs and dynamics of diverse educational environments, educators can cultivate a collaborative and supportive culture that enhances the overall quality of education.

*Promoting a sense of unity and shared purpose
among colleagues*

Fostering a sense of unity and shared purpose among colleagues is a dynamic process that requires intentional efforts, especially in times of change or uncertainty. I firmly believe that including God in this approach adds a profound dimension to the sense of unity we seek. Beyond that spiritual foundation, there are specific strategies and guidelines that have proven effective in cultivating a cohesive professional community.

First and foremost, open and transparent communication is key. During times of change or uncertainty, colleagues need to be informed and engaged in the decision-making process. Establishing a culture of open dialogue ensures that everyone feels valued and heard, contributing to a shared understanding of the goals and objectives.

Another crucial aspect is fostering a collaborative mindset. Encouraging colleagues to work together on shared projects or initiatives promotes a sense of interdependence and shared purpose. When individuals recognize their collective impact, even in the face of uncertainty, it strengthens the bonds of unity.

Acknowledging and celebrating successes, both big and small, is also instrumental. Recognizing the achievements of colleagues reinforces a positive and supportive professional culture. This practice builds a sense of collective pride and purpose, even when external circumstances may be uncertain.

In times of change, it's essential to provide opportunities for professional development and learning. Investing in the growth of colleagues demonstrates a commitment to their individual and collective success. Shared learning experiences contribute to a shared purpose and a sense of unity.

Lastly, maintaining a sense of humor and camaraderie can be a powerful tool. Laughter and shared moments of joy can help alleviate tension and create a positive atmosphere, fostering unity even in challenging times.

Ultimately, by combining these strategies with a foundation of faith and spiritual connectedness, we can navigate times of change or uncertainty with resilience and a shared sense of purpose. In doing so, we strengthen the bonds that hold our professional community together, creating a supportive and united environment.

Administrators and l leaders can facilitate a supportive and collaborative culture

Administrators and educational leaders play a pivotal role in shaping the culture of a school or educational institution. To foster a truly supportive and collaborative environment, they should prioritize several key strategies that go beyond surface-level interactions. Trust, respect, and unity must be actively cultivated rather than assumed.

First and foremost, leaders should prioritize building trust among all members of the educational community. This involves transparent communication, active listening, and a commitment to addressing concerns and feedback. When individuals feel heard and valued, trust is established, creating a foundation for collaboration.

Respect is another cornerstone of a positive culture. Administrators should model respectful behavior and set clear expectations for how everyone in the institution should treat one another. Recognizing and appreciating the diverse talents and perspectives of the staff contributes to a culture where everyone feels respected and included.

Creating opportunities for collaboration is essential. Leaders should encourage interdisciplinary teamwork, shared decision-making, and open forums for idea exchange. By fostering a collaborative spirit, administrators empower their staff to contribute to the shared goals of the institution.

Making genuine connections with staff is crucial. Leaders should take the time to understand the unique strengths and challenges of each team member. This personal touch not only enhances relationships but also contributes to a sense of belonging and commitment.

Empowering staff through leadership opportunities is a powerful way to foster collaboration. When individuals are given the chance to take on leadership roles, it not only enhances their professional growth but also creates a culture of shared responsibility and accountability.

Building staff self-esteem and knowledge should be an ongoing priority. Professional development opportunities, recognition of achievements, and a culture that values continuous learning contribute to a positive and collaborative work environment.

In summary, administrators and educational leaders can facilitate a supportive and collaborative culture by actively working on building trust, fostering respect, creating collaboration opportunities, making personal connections, empowering through leadership, and prioritizing professional development. These strategies collectively contribute to a vibrant and positive educational community where everyone is motivated to work together toward shared goals.

Scriptures That support Colleague Connections

Proverbs 27:17 (NIV): "As iron sharpens iron, so one person sharpens another."

Philippians 2:3-4 (NIV): "Do nothing out of selfish ambition or vain conceit. Rather, in humility value others above yourselves, not looking to your own interests but each of you to the interests of the others."

Ephesians 4:32 (NIV): "Be kind and compassionate to one another, forgiving each other, just as in Christ God forgave you."

Colossians 3:13 (NIV): "Bear with each other and forgive one another if any of you has a grievance against someone. Forgive as the Lord forgave you."

Proverbs 15:1 (NIV): "A gentle answer turns away wrath, but a harsh word stirs up anger."

Romans 12:10 (NIV): "Be devoted to one another in love. Honor one another above yourselves."

1 Peter 4:10 (NIV): "Each of you should use whatever gift you have received to serve others, as faithful stewards of God's grace in its various forms."

Galatians 6:2 (NIV): "Carry each other's burdens, and in this way, you will fulfill the law of Christ."

Matthew 18:20 (NIV): "For where two or three gather in my name, there am I with them."

Proverbs 12:26 (NIV): "The righteous choose their friends carefully, but the way of the wicked leads them astray."

CHAPTER 5:

Moments of Doubt: Finding Purpose and Meaning in Teaching

Moments of doubt in my teaching career,

I have personally navigated through moments of doubt in my teaching career, and these moments were particularly challenging during the early stages. At the outset, I found myself in a situation where I lacked a master's degree, unlike many of my colleagues. This disparity left me feeling inadequately equipped for the journey that lay ahead. Doubts crept in, and I began questioning whether teaching was truly my calling. I felt a sense of unease and uncertainty about whether I was on the right path.

This period of doubt led me to make the difficult decision to briefly step away from the teaching profession. I felt compelled to explore other potential callings that God might have for me. It was a soul-searching period, a quest for a deeper understanding of my purpose.

During this time, a transformative moment occurred while I was teaching in Kentucky. Overhearing a conversation about a scholarship opportunity, I recognized it as a divine intervention, a message from God guiding me toward a solution for my doubts. It became clear that pursuing a master's degree was the path I needed to take to overcome my feelings of inadequacy.

Acquiring the scholarship not only provided me with the means to further my education but also served as a confirmation of God's plan for me in the teaching profession. The doubts that once clouded my vision dissipated, replaced by a renewed sense of purpose and clarity.

This experience taught me the importance of trusting in God's guidance and being open to the unexpected ways in which He may lead us. It reinforced the idea that challenges and doubts are opportunities for growth and self-discovery. Through prayer, faith, and remaining receptive to divine interventions, I found my way back to teaching with a stronger sense of conviction and purpose than ever before.

Common triggers that lead teachers to question their purpose,

Teachers may find themselves questioning their purpose in various situations, often influenced by a combination of factors that impact their personal and professional lives. Common triggers include the level of support from family, the depth of their relationship with God, the dynamics within the classroom, the backing from the administration, financial concerns, and the overall relationships both within and outside the teaching profession.

For instance, a teacher may face challenges at home that affect their ability to fully invest in their role as an educator. Family dynamics and support play a crucial role in maintaining a teacher's sense of purpose. Similarly, the strength of one's connection with God can significantly impact resilience in the face of adversity.

The classroom environment is another critical factor. Teachers may question their purpose if they encounter persistent challenges in managing student behavior, adapting to diverse learning styles, or facing difficulties in delivering the curriculum effectively.

Administrative support is pivotal; feeling undervalued or unsupported by school leadership can lead to doubts about the meaningfulness of one's contribution. Financial pressures and struggles may also contribute to a teacher's sense of purpose being tested.

In terms of recognizing and addressing these challenges, teachers must engage in regular self-reflection. Acknowledging the impact of these triggers on their well-being and sense of purpose is the first step. Seeking support from colleagues, mentors, or mental health professionals can provide valuable perspectives and coping strategies.

Developing a strong professional network, both within and outside the school, can foster a sense of community and shared purpose. Additionally, maintaining open communication with administrators about challenges and concerns ensures that teachers feel heard and supported.

Teachers should revisit their initial calling to the profession, remembering the passion and conviction that led them to become educators. Regular prayer, seeking spiritual guidance, and staying connected with the greater purpose of education contribute to the resilience needed to navigate these challenges and rediscover meaning in their work.

Story of a teacher who have overcome doubt

Numerous teachers have faced and conquered moments of doubt, with many of these instances revolving around financial challenges. The teaching profession, despite its significant demands, often falls short in financial remuneration. This incongruity prompts teachers to weigh the pros and cons of their career, leading to the timeless question: to teach or not to teach.

Let me share a compelling story that exemplifies this struggle. Sarah, an experienced educator with a deep passion for teaching, found herself at a crossroads due to financial constraints. Balancing the demands of the classroom with the reality of limited financial rewards became a daunting task. This predicament triggered moments of doubt, making her contemplate alternative career paths.

However, Sarah's story takes an inspiring turn. Instead of succumbing to doubt and abandoning her calling, she decided to confront the financial challenges head-on. She sought additional income opportunities, such as tutoring and participating in educational programs during the summer months. Simultaneously, she engaged in open conversations with her school administration about the financial strain faced by many teachers.

Sarah's resilience and proactive approach not only improved her own financial situation but also sparked positive changes within the school. Her willingness to address the issue paved the way for a more transparent dialogue between teachers and administrators about the financial realities they faced.

This example illustrates that overcoming doubt often involves a combination of personal determination and systemic change. Teachers like Sarah, by acknowledging their doubts and actively seeking solutions, not only rediscover purpose in their work but also contribute to a broader transformation within the educational system.

Self-reflection contributes to overcoming moments of doubt

In my experience, self-reflection is an indispensable habit for any caring teacher, especially during challenging moments when it feels like it's just you and the Lord. This process plays a crucial role in decision-making and maintaining a sense of purpose. There have been numerous times when I questioned why I chose the teaching profession, considering the myriad other career paths available. However, each time I engaged in self-reflection, I rediscovered the divine calling that led me to teaching.

For teachers navigating moments of doubt, I recommend incorporating intentional self-reflection practices into your routine. Here are a few exercises that have proven effective in my own journey:

Journaling: Take time regularly to jot down your thoughts, experiences, and feelings related to teaching. Reflect on both the challenges and triumphs, allowing yourself to express the range of emotions that come with the profession.

Goal Setting: Define short-term and long-term goals for your teaching career. Reflect on how these goals align with your initial reasons for choosing this path. Regularly revisit and adjust these goals as your journey evolves.

Peer Discussions: Engage in open and honest conversations with fellow teachers. Share your doubts, concerns, and successes. Learning from others' experiences can provide valuable insights and reassurance.

Mindfulness Practices: Incorporate mindfulness techniques into your routine, such as meditation or deep breathing exercises. These practices can help you stay present, manage stress, and gain clarity during moments of uncertainty.

Seek Feedback: Actively seek feedback from students, colleagues, and mentors. Constructive feedback can offer perspectives that may not be immediately apparent, fostering growth and self-discovery.

Remember, self-reflection isn't about finding fault; it's about understanding, learning, and growing. By consistently engaging in these practices, teachers can navigate doubts, reaffirm their purpose, and find renewed meaning in their impactful profession.

Role of mentorship in helping teachers overcome moments of doubt…

Mentorship is an indispensable compass, guiding teachers through the labyrinth of doubts and uncertainties that inevitably arise in the teaching profession. Even after dedicating over 30 years to teaching, I firmly believe that seeking support from experienced colleagues is not just beneficial; it's essential.

Allow me to share a personal experience from my recent move to a new state. The educational landscape varied significantly from my previous location, and I found myself navigating through unfamiliar regulations and norms. In such moments, having a mentor became my North Star. I sought out a seasoned educator who not only understood the nuances of the educational system in the new state but also graciously shared insights, providing clarity on questions and concerns I grappled with.

This ongoing mentorship journey has been akin to having a trusted guide, someone who imparts wisdom, shares experiences, and ensures that I continually refine and perfect my craft. It's a testament to the fact that, regardless of the years devoted to teaching, there's always room to learn and grow. Seeking a mentor isn't a sign of weakness; rather, it's a proactive step towards continuous improvement.

In the tapestry of a teaching career, mentorship weaves a thread of shared experiences, guidance, and support. It's an invaluable resource that empowers educators to overcome doubts, reaffirm their purpose, and evolve in their professional journey.

Strategies or practices recommended for rediscovering joy

initially sparked our journey. During challenging times, rediscovering that joy becomes paramount. It's not a mere coincidence that the scriptures advocate for continuous learning and self-improvement. 'Study to show yourself approved' takes on profound significance in the realm of teaching. One strategy I highly recommend for reigniting the flame of joy is to delve deep into the subjects you teach. When you truly understand a concept, you develop a spirit of sharing and learning. This is the heart of teaching—a beautiful symbiosis of giving and receiving knowledge. Consider immersing yourself in continuous professional development, exploring innovative teaching methodologies, or engaging in collaborative learning communities. The more you enhance your understanding, the more invigorated your teaching becomes.

Furthermore, fostering a culture of sharing within your educational community can be a powerful practice. Encourage open dialogue, collaborative lesson planning, and knowledge exchange among colleagues. This not only enriches your own teaching experience but also contributes to a collective sense of purpose and fulfillment.

Remember, the joy of teaching is often found in the journey of discovery, both for yourself and your students. Embrace the opportunity to be both a learner and a guide, and you'll find that even in challenging times, the profound meaning of teaching is continually renewed.

Shifting your perspective during moments of doubt

In times of doubt, it's essential for teachers to navigate the storm by anchoring themselves to the positive impact they have on students and the broader community. This perspective shift is not just a mindset but a deliberate and transformative practice.

Teachers, especially those who feel a divine calling, understand that the essence of their role is deeply intertwined with the lives of their students. Here are some actionable strategies to solidify this perspective:

Reflect on Success Stories: Take a moment to reflect on the success stories of your students. Recall instances where you witnessed their growth, understanding, or even a spark of inspiration. These stories are powerful reminders of the lasting impact you can have.

Create an 'Impact Wall': Designate a space in your classroom or workspace to create an 'Impact Wall.' Pin letters, drawings, or notes from students expressing gratitude or showcasing their achievements. This tangible display serves as a visual testament to the positive influence you've had.

Engage with the Community: Extend your perspective beyond the classroom. Engage with the broader community to witness firsthand the ripple effect of education. Attend community events, collaborate with local organizations, or involve students in community service projects. Seeing your influence extend beyond the classroom can be a profound motivator.

Establish Mentorship Connections: Connect with veteran teachers or mentors who can share their own experiences of doubt and renewal. Learning from their journeys and seeking guidance can provide invaluable insights into maintaining a positive perspective.

Daily Gratitude Practice: Incorporate a daily gratitude practice into your routine. Before or after each school day, jot down one thing you're grateful for in your teaching experience. This simple ritual can shift your focus towards the positive aspects of your profession.

Remember, doubt is a natural part of any meaningful journey. By actively and intentionally focusing on the positive impact you have on students and the community, you not only weather moments of doubt but also reaffirm the profound purpose and meaning inherent in the teaching profession.

Advice for educators facing pressures of doubt about their profession?

When educators find themselves grappling with external pressures or navigating through challenging changes that sow seeds of doubt, it's crucial to reconnect with the core reasons that led them to choose teaching as their profession. Here's some actionable advice to guide educators in overcoming these hurdles:

Revisit Your Why: Take a moment to reflect on the initial reasons that inspired you to become an educator. What ignited your passion for teaching? Write down these motivations and keep them as a reminder in your workspace. Reconnecting with your 'why' can reignite the flame that brought you into this profession.

Seek Supportive Networks: Reach out to colleagues, mentors, or professional networks. Sharing experiences and concerns with others in the field can provide valuable perspectives and insights. Sometimes, knowing that others face similar challenges can be reassuring and offer a sense of solidarity.

Set Realistic Expectations: Assess the external pressures you're facing and evaluate if the expectations placed upon you are realistic and achievable. If there are unrealistic demands, consider having a constructive conversation with administrators or supervisors about finding a balanced approach that aligns with both your well-being and professional responsibilities.

Professional Development: Invest time in professional development opportunities. This could involve attending workshops, webinars, or conferences that focus on strategies for coping with external pressures, adapting to changes, and maintaining a healthy work-life balance.

Mindfulness and Self-Care: Incorporate mindfulness practices and self-care routines into your daily life. Techniques like meditation, deep breathing, or simply taking short breaks during the day can help alleviate stress and foster a more positive outlook.

Embrace Flexibility: Understand that change is inevitable, and flexibility is a valuable skill. Embrace adaptability and view challenges as opportunities for growth. A flexible mindset enables educators to navigate uncertainties with resilience.

Remember, doubt is a common companion on the journey of any meaningful profession. By actively addressing these external pressures and proactively engaging with supportive strategies, educators can rekindle their sense of purpose and find renewed meaning in their vital role.

Creating a supportive environment

In fostering a supportive environment that not only acknowledges but actively addresses moments of doubt among teachers, administrators and educational leaders play a pivotal role. Here are concrete strategies to make this support more robust and meaningful:

Transparent Leadership: Administrators should practice transparent leadership by openly sharing their own experiences of doubt and the strategies they've employed to overcome them. This vulnerability fosters a culture of openness and understanding, reassuring teachers that doubts are a natural part of the profession.

Regular Check-Ins: Establish a system of regular check-ins where administrators engage in one-on-one conversations with teachers. This provides a dedicated space for teachers to express concerns, share doubts, and receive personalized support. Consistent communication helps build trust and strengthens the teacher-administrator relationship.

Professional Development Opportunities: Offer targeted professional development sessions that address common challenges causing moments of doubt. This could include workshops on managing stress, adapting to new teaching methodologies, or sessions focused on personal well-being. These opportunities demonstrate a commitment to teachers' continuous growth.

Peer Mentorship Programs: Implement peer mentorship programs where experienced teachers, who may have navigated through doubt themselves, can offer guidance and support to their colleagues. This creates a sense of community and allows teachers to learn from each other's experiences.

Resource Allocation: Ensure teachers have access to resources that facilitate their professional and personal development. This might involve investing in books, online courses, or workshops that specifically target areas causing doubt. Providing tangible support demonstrates a commitment to teachers' success.

Recognition and Appreciation: Acknowledge and celebrate teachers' achievements, both big and small. Recognizing their efforts and contributions reinforces their sense of purpose and helps counter moments of doubt. Simple gestures of appreciation, such as shout-outs in staff meetings or small awards, can go a long way.

Establish a Supportive Culture: Cultivate a school culture that prioritizes mental health and well-being. Encourage teachers to take breaks when needed, practice self-care, and create a culture where it's acceptable to seek help. This requires a proactive approach to dismantling stigmas around vulnerability.

By adopting these strategies, administrators and educational leaders can actively contribute to a supportive environment where teachers feel heard, valued, and equipped to navigate moments of doubt with resilience.

Embracing the purpose contributes to overcoming doubts

In my perspective, teaching transcends being just a profession; it's a divine calling bestowed upon us by God. Embracing the profound and broader purpose of education is not merely about imparting knowledge but fulfilling a higher calling. This recognition can be a cornerstone in overcoming doubts and finding enduring meaning in the teaching profession.

Understanding that we play a vital role in shaping not just academic minds but contributing to the moral and spiritual development of our students adds a profound layer of significance to our work. By viewing education as a conduit for fostering empathy, critical thinking, and moral values, we tap into a purpose that extends far beyond the classroom walls.

Teachers become agents of positive change, influencing the future generation in ways that can have a lasting impact on society. Recognizing the transformative power of education helps us navigate through moments of doubt. It allows us to see beyond immediate challenges, finding solace and inspiration in the greater purpose we serve.

Moreover, embracing the broader purpose of education instills a sense of responsibility and accountability. It prompts us to continually reflect on our teaching methods, strive for excellence, and seek continuous improvement. This commitment to a higher purpose becomes a guiding light during times of uncertainty, reaffirming our dedication to the noble calling of teaching.

Viewing education as a divine calling and recognizing its broader purpose not only elevates the significance of our profession but becomes a source of enduring motivation, resilience, and fulfillment, even in the face of doubts.

These questions aim to draw out personal experiences, practical strategies, and words of encouragement from Dr.

Dayse, offering readers insights and guidance on navigating and overcoming moments of doubt in their teaching careers.

Scriptures That support Moments of Doubt

Isaiah 41:10 (NIV): "So do not fear, for I am with you; do not be dismayed, for I am your God. I will strengthen you and help you; I will uphold you with my righteous right hand."

Philippians 4:13 (NIV): "I can do all this through him who gives me strength."

Jeremiah 29:11 (NIV): "For I know the plans I have for you, declares the Lord, plans for welfare and not for evil, to give you a future and a hope."

Psalm 34:17-18 (NIV): "The righteous cry out, and the Lord hears them; he delivers them from all their troubles. The Lord is close to the brokenhearted and saves those who are crushed in spirit."

2 Corinthians 12:9 (NIV): "But he said to me, 'My grace is sufficient for you, for my power is made perfect in weakness.' Therefore, I will boast all the

more gladly about my weaknesses, so that Christ's power may rest on me."

Psalm 23:1-4 (NIV): "The Lord is my shepherd, I lack nothing. He makes me lie down in green pastures, he leads me beside quiet waters, he refreshes my soul. He guides me along the right paths for his name's sake. Even though I walk through the darkest valley, I will fear no evil, for you are with me; your rod and your staff, they comfort me."

Proverbs 3:5-6 (NIV): "Trust in the Lord with all your heart and lean not on your own understanding; in all your ways submit to him, and he will make your paths straight."

Psalm 94:19 (NIV): "When anxiety was great within me, your consolation brought me joy."

Matthew 11:28-30 (NIV): "Come to me, all you who are weary and burdened, and I will give you rest. Take my yoke upon you and learn from me, for I am gentle and humble in heart, and you will find rest for your souls. For my yoke is easy and my burden is light."

Romans 8:28 (NIV): "And we know that in all things God works for the good of those who love him, who have been called according to his purpose."

CHAPTER 6,

Faith in the Classroom: Integrating Faith and Education

Integrating your faith into your teaching practices,

Incorporating faith into my daily teaching practices is not just a ritual but a profound source of strength and guidance that shapes my approach to education. Each new day in the classroom is an unpredictable journey, and having a deep connection with God is my anchor. This connection is nurtured through prayer warriors, dedicated time for scripture reading, and the application of spiritual insights to the challenges of the classroom.

The impact of integrating faith into my teaching extends far beyond the academic realm. It's a transformative force that resonates in the learning environment and touches the lives of my students. By consistently relying on my faith, I'm able to navigate the unpredictable nature of teaching with a sense of purpose, resilience, and unwavering hope.

There have been numerous instances where referring to my faith became a guiding light in moments of uncertainty. The ability to turn to God for direction and leadership has not only provided a personal sanctuary but has also translated into a positive and nurturing atmosphere for my students. The learning environment becomes a space where not only academic growth, but also spiritual and emotional well-being are fostered.

If I hadn't cultivated and relied on my faith, the challenges of the teaching profession might have led me to a different path. My recommendation to fellow teachers is to seek something profound to believe in, to anchor themselves amidst the storms of education. Connecting with a church community and actively nurturing your faith can be a transformative journey that not only sustains your personal and professional life but creates a ripple effect of positivity and resilience in the lives of your students.

Incorporating faith-based elements

While I haven't explicitly incorporated faith-based lessons into my curriculum due to the strict guidelines of public-school districts, I can attest that the essence of my teaching, including patience and the lessons themselves, is deeply influenced and inspired by my faith in God. As a former social studies teacher, I've navigated topics within World Studies that naturally include discussions about God.

Even though I couldn't directly introduce faith-based elements into the lesson plans, I've had students inquire about God during class discussions. In such instances, I've delicately directed them to their parents or suggested seeking guidance from a clergy member. Public school regulations emphasize the importance of maintaining a neutral stance on religious matters, which I respect and adhere to.

Despite the limitations imposed by these guidelines, my teaching philosophy is inherently rooted in my spiritual beliefs. The challenges and triumphs that arise in the classroom are approached with the patience, compassion, and wisdom that I draw from my faith. While I may not explicitly bring God into the classroom, the spirit of my teaching reflects the inspiration derived from my spiritual journey.

It's a delicate balance, respecting the boundaries set by the school district while infusing my lessons with the values and virtues instilled by my faith. This approach not only aligns with professional standards but also allows me to create an environment where students can witness the positive impact of faith in action without breaching any established guidelines.

Balancing diverse beliefs and backgrounds

In my extensive experience as an educator, navigating the diverse beliefs and backgrounds of students has been a longstanding challenge, but it has evolved in contemporary times. Unlike the past, today, a significant number of parents are not actively instilling religious teachings in their children, and a growing proportion of students are not being raised within the church.

This shift in religious upbringing has undoubtedly impacted the educational experience. Students, often lacking a foundation in religious principles, may face challenges in making morally sound decisions. Unlike an era when religious values were more universally respected, the current landscape demands a nuanced approach to integrating faith into the educational experience.

As educators, it becomes crucial for us to recognize and respect the diverse beliefs present in our classrooms. While it may be tempting to directly integrate faith-based elements into lessons, it's essential to acknowledge the changing landscape and tailor our approach accordingly. Rather than assuming a universal understanding of religious principles, we must foster an environment that encourages open discussions about diverse perspectives.

One effective strategy is to incorporate lessons that promote moral and ethical decision-making without explicitly relying on religious doctrines. This not only respects the diverse beliefs of students but also helps instill valuable principles that transcend specific religious affiliations.

Moreover, educators can actively engage with students on a personal level, encouraging them to share their beliefs and backgrounds. This fosters an inclusive atmosphere where diverse perspectives are not only acknowledged but celebrated. By creating a space for open dialogue, we can bridge the gap created by varying religious upbringings and help students form their moral compass.

Navigating the complexities of diverse beliefs in today's educational landscape requires a thoughtful and adaptable approach. By recognizing the changes in religious practices and embracing a more inclusive framework, educators can still integrate faith into the educational experience in a meaningful and respectful manner.

Moments of reflection in a spiritually enriching classroom environment

Prayer is not just a routine; it's a powerful force that profoundly influences the dynamics within a classroom. Moments of reflection and prayer hold a pivotal role in shaping not only the teacher's attitude but also the overall environment and, most importantly, the students' perspectives.

Consider prayer as the invisible architect constructing a foundation for a spiritually enriching classroom. It goes beyond the tangible and ushers in an intangible, yet palpable, atmosphere of serenity and safety. It's the unspoken reassurance that envelops the classroom, creating a haven for learning.

In these moments of reflection, we tap into a dimension that transcends the physical realm. It's a collective experience where, although unseen, the impact is felt by everyone present. It transforms the mundane into the sacred, setting the tone for meaningful interactions and fostering an environment where the spirit of learning can thrive.

When we engage in prayer within the classroom, we're not just going through the motions. It's a deliberate act to invite positivity, understanding, and a sense of unity. Students, often facing challenges beyond the classroom, find solace in this shared moment of reflection. It becomes a sanctuary where they can momentarily escape the pressures of the external world and immerse themselves in an environment of acceptance and support.

These prayer moments are the catalysts for an educational sanctuary — a place where the spiritual and the academic seamlessly intertwine. As we may not always see the impact with our physical eyes, the transformative power of these moments is evident in the positive shifts in attitude, the fostering of a safe haven for students, and the intangible but unmistakable difference in the overall classroom ambiance.

Addressing potential challenges regarding the integration of faith in the classroom

Addressing potential challenges or concerns regarding the integration of faith in the classroom is not just a task; it's a spiritual journey that begins with a foundation of prayer. As educators, we embark on each school day with an acknowledgment that challenges may arise, but we are fortified with a profound sense of divine guidance.

Commencing the day with prayer serves as our compass, ensuring that we are attuned to the spiritual realm, ready to navigate any concerns that may come our way. It's more than a routine; it's a deliberate act of surrender, inviting a divine presence into the classroom.

When confronted with challenges from students, parents, or colleagues, our reliance on prayer becomes our unwavering strength. It's the assurance that we are not alone in addressing these concerns — that we have sought divine wisdom and protection before stepping into the realm of education.

This spiritual preparation enables us to respond with a calm and understanding demeanor. The challenges, though varied, are met with a resilience derived from a connection to something greater than ourselves. In moments of uncertainty, we draw from the patience and understanding granted by the divine, navigating challenges not merely as individuals but as conduits for a higher purpose.

Prayer becomes our shield, protecting us from doubt and strengthening our resolve to integrate faith seamlessly into the educational environment. It transforms challenges into opportunities for growth, fostering an atmosphere where concerns are met with compassion, understanding, and the wisdom bestowed upon us through our spiritual journey.

The integration of faith is not a source of contention but a harmonious blend that enriches the educational experience. By starting each day with a prayerful heart, we ensure that the challenges become steppingstones rather than stumbling blocks, creating a classroom environment where faith and education coexist harmoniously.

Fostering spiritual development among students?

The effectiveness of fostering spiritual development among students transcends traditional teaching methods; it's a fusion of professional preparedness and spiritual presence that leaves an indelible mark from the very first interaction. Beyond lesson plans and educational strategies, the teacher's authenticity becomes the beacon guiding students toward spiritual growth.

Being prepared professionally is not merely about delivering curriculum; it's about embodying a commitment to excellence in education. When students witness this commitment, it sets the stage for a transformative educational experience. They perceive dedication and passion that goes beyond the surface, sparking a curiosity about what sets the teacher apart.

Simultaneously, the spiritual preparedness of the teacher becomes the silent force that speaks volumes in the classroom. It's an intangible quality that students pick up on, creating an environment where they feel a sense of safety and genuine care. This spiritual presence isn't overt but subtly influences the atmosphere, fostering a sense of purpose and connection.

Beyond conventional teaching approaches, the teacher's demeanor, words, and actions become the curriculum for spiritual development. The teacher is not just an instructor of subjects; they become a guide on a shared journey of self-discovery and spiritual exploration.

In this context, the classroom transforms into a sacred space where education transcends textbooks, and spiritual development becomes an inherent part of the learning process. The impact is profound, as students not only absorb academic knowledge but also witness the embodiment of values, compassion, and a higher purpose.

Ultimately, the most effective teaching method for fostering spiritual development is the marriage of professional excellence and spiritual authenticity. It's the recognition that education is not just about filling minds with information but nurturing souls with wisdom, kindness, and a profound sense of purpose.

Creating a classroom culture that respects and
values diverse spiritual perspectives

Educators hold the key to cultivating a classroom culture that not only respects but values the rich tapestry of diverse spiritual perspectives present among students. The task at hand involves a delicate dance of inclusivity, fostering an environment where faith-based principles seamlessly integrate with the varied beliefs represented in the classroom.

The cornerstone of this approach lies in fostering open-mindedness and understanding. Educators serve as facilitators of dialogue, encouraging students to share and appreciate the unique spiritual perspectives they bring to the learning space. By creating an atmosphere of mutual respect, students can engage in meaningful conversations that broaden their understanding of different faiths.

Furthermore, incorporating diverse perspectives into the curriculum becomes an integral part of this process. Educators can introduce literature, historical events, or philosophical discussions that highlight the richness of various spiritual traditions. This not only adds depth to the academic experience but also promotes a sense of interconnectedness among students.

Balancing this inclusivity with the integration of faith-based principles involves a nuanced approach. Educators can draw upon universal values that transcend specific religious doctrines, emphasizing concepts like kindness, empathy, and compassion. By focusing on these shared principles, educators create a common ground that unites students regardless of their individual spiritual backgrounds.

It's crucial for educators to model the respect and understanding they aim to instill in their students. Embracing their own spiritual authenticity without imposing it on others sets a powerful example. This transparency fosters an environment where students feel safe expressing their beliefs, knowing that differences are not just tolerated but celebrated.

Creating a classroom culture that harmonizes diverse spiritual perspectives with faith-based principles is an ongoing journey. It requires intentional efforts, genuine conversations, and a commitment to building bridges of understanding among students.

Through this approach, educators become architects of a learning environment that not only imparts knowledge but also nurtures the spirit of unity in diversity.

Integration of faith contributes to a sense of purpose

The seamless integration of faith into the educational fabric serves as a transformative force, ushering in a profound sense of purpose and fulfillment for both educators and students. At its core, this integration becomes a guiding light, illuminating the path toward holistic development and a deeper understanding of one's place in the world.

For educators, the integration of faith breathes life into their professional journey. It transforms the act of teaching from a mere profession to a divine calling, instilling a profound sense of purpose that transcends the boundaries of the classroom. When educators recognize their role as stewards of knowledge and spiritual guides, each lesson becomes a sacred endeavor to nurture minds, hearts, and souls.

Simultaneously, students find themselves on a journey of self-discovery that extends beyond academic achievements. The integration of faith fosters an environment where curiosity meets spirituality, where the pursuit of knowledge becomes a quest for deeper meaning. Students are not just recipients of information but active participants in a transformative process that shapes their character and worldview.

Moreover, the integration of faith provides a moral compass that guides decision-making and interpersonal relationships. It cultivates virtues such as empathy, compassion, and humility, fostering a sense of community within the classroom. Students learn not only academic subjects but also the invaluable lessons of integrity, kindness, and respect for others.

The fulfillment derived from this integration extends beyond the walls of the classroom, permeating every aspect of life. It empowers educators and students alike to navigate challenges with resilience, viewing setbacks as opportunities for growth and learning. The sense of purpose becomes a driving force that transcends the ordinary, infusing each day with significance and impact.

In essence, the integration of faith in education weaves a tapestry of purpose and fulfillment that extends far beyond academic achievements. It becomes a transformative force that shapes character, builds community, and imparts enduring values. For both educators and students, it is not merely an addition to the curriculum but a source of inspiration that enriches the educational experience and contributes to a more profound understanding of life's purpose.

Guidance on navigating potential legal or policy considerations

Addressing the delicate balance between faith and public-school settings requires a nuanced approach, considering the legal and policy considerations that govern the separation of church and state. While it's essential to respect these boundaries, there are ways to authentically integrate faith without infringing on established regulations.

First and foremost, educators must be well-versed in the legal landscape that governs their profession. Understanding the parameters of the law ensures that any integration of faith remains within acceptable boundaries. This knowledge empowers educators to navigate potential legal considerations with confidence and clarity.

Furthermore, it's crucial to focus on the values and universal principles that transcend specific religious affiliations. Emphasizing virtues such as compassion, empathy, and respect creates a moral foundation that aligns with broader ethical standards. This approach allows for the integration of universally accepted principles without favoring any particular religious doctrine.

When engaging in discussions or activities that touch upon faith-related topics, it's beneficial to foster an inclusive environment. Encourage open dialogue that respects diverse perspectives and beliefs, creating a space where students feel free to express their views without fear of judgment. This approach aligns with the principles of tolerance and diversity, promoting an atmosphere of mutual respect.

Moreover, collaboration with school administrators and legal experts can provide valuable insights into the specific policies and guidelines applicable to the educational institution. Establishing a dialogue ensures that any integration of faith aligns with the institution's mission and values while adhering to legal requirements.

The key is to approach the integration of faith in a thoughtful and inclusive manner. By prioritizing values that resonate across different belief systems and staying informed about legal considerations, educators can create an environment that acknowledges spirituality without overstepping established boundaries. This approach allows for the meaningful integration of faith while maintaining the integrity and legality of the educational setting.

Hesitant about incorporating faith?

Embracing the integration of faith into teaching practices can be a transformative journey, but it's understandable that educators may harbor hesitations or uncertainties. My advice to educators contemplating this path is to authentically be themselves and let the light of their faith shine through in their interactions with students, colleagues, and within the broader community.

Firstly, it's essential to recognize that incorporating faith into teaching practices doesn't necessarily mean imposing personal beliefs on others. Instead, it involves embodying the values and principles that guide one's faith in a way that is inclusive, respectful, and reflective of universal virtues.

To embark on this journey, educators should start by reflecting on their own beliefs and identifying the core values they wish to exemplify. Whether it's compassion, kindness, or empathy, these universal principles can serve as a foundation for integrating faith without alienating those with different beliefs.

Being genuine and transparent about one's faith journey can foster connections with students and parents. Share personal stories or experiences that highlight the positive impact faith has had on your life. This authenticity can build trust and understanding, creating a more open and receptive environment.

It's important to approach this integration with sensitivity, respecting the diverse backgrounds and beliefs present in the educational setting. Focus on creating an inclusive space where students feel valued regardless of their faith or background. This involves being mindful of language, activities, and discussions to ensure they are respectful of everyone's perspectives.

For educators who may be unsure about the boundaries, seeking guidance from school administrators, mentors, or legal experts can provide clarity. Understanding the specific policies and regulations governing the educational institution will help educators navigate the integration of faith within established parameters.

Ultimately, incorporating faith into teaching practices is a personal journey, and educators should feel empowered to explore this path in a way that aligns with their values and the broader mission of education. By embracing authenticity, inclusivity, and a commitment to universal virtues, educators can create a meaningful and fulfilling teaching experience for themselves and their students.

Scriptures that support Integrating Faith and Education

Proverbs 22:6 (NIV): "Start children off on the way they should go, and even when they are old, they will not turn from it."

Deuteronomy 6:6-7 (NIV): "These commandments that I give you today are to be on your hearts. Impress them on your children. Talk about them when you sit at home and when you walk along the road, when you lie down and when you get up."

Colossians 3:23 (NIV): "Whatever you do, work at it with all your heart, as working for the Lord, not for human masters."

2 Timothy 3:16-17 (NIV): "All Scripture is God-breathed and is useful for teaching, rebuking, correcting and training in righteousness, so that the servant of God may be thoroughly equipped for every good work."

Matthew 5:16 (NIV): "In the same way, let your light shine before others, that they may see your good deeds and glorify your Father in heaven."

Philippians 4:8 (NIV): "Finally, brothers and sisters, whatever is true, whatever is noble, whatever is right, whatever is pure, whatever is lovely, whatever is admirable—if anything is excellent or praiseworthy—think about such things."

Psalm 119:105 (NIV): "Your word is a lamp for my feet, a light on my path."

John 14:26 (NIV): "But the Advocate, the Holy Spirit, whom the Father will send in my name, will teach you all things and will remind you of everything I have said to you."

1 Corinthians 10:31 (NIV): "So whether you eat or drink or whatever you do, do it all for the glory of God."

Ephesians 6:4 (NIV): "Fathers, do not exasperate your children; instead, bring them up in the training and instruction of the Lord."

These scriptures can serve as a foundation for discussing the integration of faith into teaching practices and emphasizing the spiritual aspects of education. They highlight the importance of aligning teaching with biblical principles and promoting a positive, values-based learning environment.

CHAPTER 7:

Inspiring Students Success: Making a Lasting Impact

In this section teachers and school administrators share a personal story or example of a teacher who made a significant and lasting impact on your own life.

Joyce Bell Murphy, MAT, ED.S who has spent over 20 years in education with learning disabilities K-12, worked as an adjunct professor, co-director, and academic advisor in secondary education. Currently retired. Says: "One teacher who profoundly influenced my life was Miss Patricia Tate, my second-grade teacher. I vividly recall a moment when a new math concept left me feeling utterly lost and frustrated. Unable to grasp the intricacies, I went home in tears, seeking solace from my mother.

In an extraordinary display of dedication, Miss Tate didn't confine her teaching to the classroom. My mother reached out to her, and without hesitation, Miss Tate invited us into her home. Picture this – sitting at her living room table, surrounded by an atmosphere of warmth and encouragement. Patiently, she took me through each step of the math problems, unraveling the complexities until I grasped the concept.

What struck me most was not just her teaching prowess but her genuine commitment to the success of every student. This experience wasn't isolated to me; Miss Tate extended her unwavering support to all her students. Her dedication went beyond the call of duty, leaving an indelible mark on my educational journey.

Miss Tate's actions taught me the true essence of teaching – a commitment to students' success that transcends the confines of a classroom. Her selfless dedication fostered an environment where students felt valued, supported, and capable of overcoming any challenge.

Even in my career as an educator, Miss Tate's influence remains a guiding light. Her legacy serves as a reminder of the profound impact a teacher can have on a student's life, shaping not just academic understanding but instilling confidence and resilience. Miss Tate's commitment to her students is a beacon of inspiration, reminding us all of the transformative power of dedicated educators."

Sylvia Williams Tompkins, M.Ed., is a certified 9-12 Business Education, who worked her way from the business arena back into the classroom. Born in a small town, Greenwood, SC and worked as a business education teacher until her retirement with Charlotte Mecklenburg Schools. Says: "The teacher who left an indelible mark on my life was Mrs. Henrietta Williams, my 2nd-grade teacher at East End Elementary school in Greenwood, SC. Mrs. Williams embodied qualities that transcended the traditional role of a teacher. Her firmness wasn't just about maintaining order; it reflected her genuine care for each student's well-being.

What set Mrs. Williams apart was her unwavering commitment to ensuring every student understood their assignments. If confusion lingered, she didn't hesitate to revisit the material, patiently explaining until clarity dawned. This dedication extended beyond the classroom; Mrs. Williams fostered strong connections with parents. By involving parents in their children's education, she created a collaborative environment that supported students both in and out of school.

Reflecting on Mrs. Williams' impact, I believe certain qualities and practices define a truly impactful teacher. Foremost is honesty – an openness that allows students to trust and connect with their teacher. Mrs. Williams exemplified this quality, creating an environment where students felt safe to learn, ask questions, and grow.

Equally significant was her genuine care. Mrs. Williams went beyond the academic realm; she cared about our overall well-being. This investment in each student's success created a lasting impression. I distinctly remember moments when, after struggling with an assignment, a revelation occurred. Mrs. Williams celebrated these 'aha' moments with us, reinforcing the fact that learning is not just about meeting academic standards but about understanding and applying knowledge.

The impact of such experiences lingers in a student's memory. I believe that the moments when a teacher's dedication unlocks understanding are the ones that stay with students throughout their lives. Mrs. Williams' teaching philosophy, grounded in care, honesty, and fostering understanding, has become a guiding principle in my own educational journey.

In her legacy, Mrs. Williams reminds us that impactful teaching is not just about disseminating information; it's about cultivating an environment where every student can thrive, experience those enlightening moments, and carry the lessons forward into a brighter future."

Ann Wagner, M.Ed., is a retired, K-12 certified teacher from Nashua, NH, has dedicated over 40 years of her life to the education profession as a Special educator. Married to a military officer, Ann has traveled throughout the world and has been an advocate for children and adults both in the United States and Europe. Says: "The best teacher I've ever known isn't just a professional educator; she's, my sister. Throughout her career, she devoted her life to the noble profession of teaching, specializing in working with students facing significant challenges. Her impact extended beyond the classroom, as she became a beacon of hope and progress for countless lives.

What set my sister apart was her unwavering commitment to improving the quality of her students' lives. Despite the significant challenges they faced, she held high expectations for each one. Witnessing her blend of patience, determination, and an innate ability to connect with students was truly remarkable. Teaching seemed to come naturally to her, and her retirement left behind a legacy of countless classrooms filled with happy students, each prepared for the journey of life.

Reflecting on her impactful teaching, certain qualities and practices stand out. Honesty was the cornerstone of her approach – she believed in being transparent with her students, setting clear expectations, and fostering an environment of trust. Compassion guided her every interaction, making her students feel seen, heard, and valued.

Clear expectations were not just about academic standards but about instilling a sense of purpose and responsibility. Kindness was a prevailing theme in her classrooms, creating a nurturing atmosphere where students felt safe to learn and grow. Patience, an essential virtue, allowed her to navigate challenges with grace and perseverance.

Prayer was a source of strength for her. In moments of difficulty, she turned to her faith, finding guidance and resilience. Her good and loving heart shone through every interaction, leaving an enduring impact on those she taught.

One particular anecdote that stands out is her love for her profession. In that moment, I witnessed firsthand the transformative power of my sister's teaching. It encapsulated the qualities that make a teacher impactful and memorable – a blend of honesty, compassion, clear expectations, kindness, patience, prayer, and a genuinely good and loving heart.

In honoring my sister's legacy, I am reminded that teaching is not just a profession; it's a calling to make a positive difference in the lives of others. Her unwavering dedication has left an indelible mark on countless students, demonstrating the profound impact a teacher can have when driven by love, compassion, and a commitment to nurturing the potential within each student."

Gayle Hutcherson, M.A, retired AB French, Spanish, and Teacher Mentor with Lexington Public School System in Lexington, KY, have dedicated 40+years of teaching children foreign languages and English as a Second Language has been Nominated: Who's Who in High School Teachers (7 times) by students, says: "My journey in education spans over 40 years, dedicating my passion to teaching foreign languages and English as a Second Language. Amidst this rewarding career, a pivotal moment stands out— the impact of my high school French 4 teacher, Mme. Hogan.

In those formative years, Mme. Hogan recognized a potential in me that I was neglecting. Despite my laziness in learning, she saw beyond and knew I could do better. Surprisingly, she awarded me a B, not as a punitive measure, but as a powerful lesson—she believed in my capacity and wanted me to realize the importance of working to one's full potential. This experience, initially sparking frustration, ultimately instilled in me a valuable life lesson about the significance of striving for excellence.

The phrase 'They don't care how much you know until you show them how much you care' has become a cliché for a reason. Students remember educators who make them feel cared for. Recently, I experienced the profound impact of this truth when I lost a student from two decades ago to sickle cell anemia. To my surprise, he revealed that I was the only teacher who truly cared about him throughout his academic journey. While I humbly doubt being the sole caring influence, his words underscore the fact that many educators struggle to convey genuine care. Those who succeed in doing so become truly memorable to their students.

Caring isn't just a sentiment; it's a practice that requires intentionality. It involves understanding each student's unique needs, challenges, and aspirations. Differentiating instruction and assignments play a crucial role in this process. Recognizing and embracing diverse learning styles is paramount to keeping students engaged and ensuring that education resonates with them personally.

In my decades of teaching, Mme. Hogan's lessons and the realization of the impact of genuine care have been guiding principles. As educators, we have the privilege and responsibility to shape not just academic futures, but also the character and self-belief of our students. Mme. Hogan's insight continues to inspire my approach, reminding me of the profound influence a teacher can have on a student's journey toward realizing their full potential."

Charlene White Reese, M.Ed., has spent over 15 years as a high school Business Education Teacher in South Carolina public schools. Her children, Shawndora, Bernard, Christopher and Chyna inspired her to continue her calling. She says: "High school was the turning point where I encountered a teacher whose influence has shaped my adult life — Ms. A.K. McGriff, my 10th-grade English teacher. Rumors preceded her, depicting a strict and proper educator who adhered to the book. On the first day, the tension was palpable, and she gave students the chance to switch classes if her approach wasn't to our liking. Many chose to leave, but fearing my mother's reaction, I stayed.

As the initial fear subsided, I began to understand Ms. McGriff's intentions. Her strictness wasn't about control but a deep desire for our success in the real world. I realized this might be a unique opportunity for personal and academic growth. I grew to love her commitment to molding students into resilient individuals. She became my mentor, a woman of class and dignity who never looked down on me.

When I later navigated a predominantly white college, Ms. McGriff was my guardian angel through the transition. Her impact endured even after her passing in 2006, remaining my guiding light. The qualities that, in my view, define a truly memorable and impactful teacher are honesty and an understanding of students' social needs. Many students grapple with social issues that must be addressed before meaningful engagement in the classroom can occur.

During the pivotal interaction between teacher and student, a relationship must be cultivated. While not every connection will flourish, as long as the teacher has been honest and worked to establish a comfortable learning environment, they can rest assured they've done their best. In education, there's no one-size-fits-all approach, emphasizing the importance of individualized care and attention."

Sandra Baker-Wilson, E.DS, DD, a former public-school administrator, dedicated over 20 years of her life to educating children in Kentucky, Georgia, and Mississippi. Her journey into education wasn't initially apparent, but her mother, a teacher, served as a source of inspiration, revealing how her talents could make a meaningful impact in the field.

As she embraced the calling to teach, Dr. Baker-Wilson found profound fulfillment in witnessing students, particularly those with past trauma or emotional struggles, overcome adversity. Their success stories, graduating from high school or college and becoming productive citizens, became the pinnacle of her educational journey.

Upon retiring from teaching and administration, she embarked on a second calling as a full-time minister in the United Methodist Church. Acknowledging that this path wasn't without challenges, Dr. Baker-Wilson was guided by the belief instilled by her mother, trusting that it was the direction God intended for her.

In reflecting on what makes a memorable teacher, Dr. Baker-Wilson emphasizes qualities of honesty, directness with students, and allowing God to lead them as they guide children."

Balancing academic rigor with creating a nurturing and inspiring atmosphere

In reflecting on the experiences shared by educators in this section, a common thread emerges—the ability to strike a harmonious balance between academic rigor and the creation of a nurturing and inspiring atmosphere for students. What stands out are two key ingredients that these remarkable teachers consistently embody: a profound love for their craft and an unwavering sense of motivation.

These teachers, rooted in their faith and possessing a deep knowledge of their content areas, exemplify a commitment to continuous learning and sharing of best practices. Drawing inspiration from their spiritual connection, each educator has developed a unique instructional style, marked by a keen understanding of how to differentiate instruction to meet the diverse needs of their students.

To illustrate, let's explore the narratives of these teachers in action. For instance, Teacher A, driven by a genuine passion for their subject, implemented project-based learning initiatives that not only challenged students academically but also fostered a sense of creativity and collaboration within the classroom. Meanwhile, Teacher B, motivated by a profound dedication to their students' well-being, integrated regular check-ins, and reflective exercises into their curriculum, creating an atmosphere where students felt seen, valued, and inspired to excel.

Examples of specific strategies to inspire and empower students

There exists a rich tapestry of strategies that teachers can employ to not only inspire but also empower their students to reach their fullest potential. Let's delve into a few illustrative examples that showcase the diversity of approaches available:

Personalized Learning Plans: Tailoring instruction to individual student needs is a potent strategy. By assessing each student's strengths, weaknesses, and learning styles, teachers can create personalized learning plans. For instance, Teacher A regularly conducts learning style assessments and adjusts instructional methods, accordingly, ensuring that each student receives targeted support.

Project-Based Learning Initiatives: Engaging students in real-world, hands-on projects fosters a sense of purpose and autonomy. Teacher B, for instance, incorporates project-based learning into the curriculum, challenging students to apply theoretical knowledge to practical scenarios. This not only enhances their understanding but also instills a sense of accomplishment.

Mentorship Programs: Establishing mentorship programs can have a profound impact. Teacher C has implemented a peer mentoring system where older students guide and support younger ones. This not only creates a supportive community but also encourages a sense of responsibility and leadership among students.

Goal Setting and Reflection: Encouraging students to set personal and academic goals provides direction and motivation. Teacher D incorporates regular goal-setting sessions into the classroom routine, allowing students to articulate their aspirations and track their progress. Reflection exercises at the end of each term help them celebrate achievements and identify areas for growth.

Incorporating Technology: Leveraging technology can enhance engagement and open up new avenues for learning. Teacher E integrates interactive online platforms and virtual field trips into the curriculum, sparking enthusiasm and curiosity among students.

These examples underscore the versatility of strategies available to educators. By adopting a combination of these approaches or tailoring them to suit the unique needs of their students, teachers can create an environment where inspiration and empowerment become guiding principles in every student's educational journey.

Role of mentorship, and how educators serve as mentors

Mentorship is a powerful force that can leave a lasting impact on students, shaping not only their academic journey but also their personal development. Educators have a unique opportunity to serve as mentors and guide students on their path to success. Here's a closer look at the role of mentorship and how educators can be effective mentors:

Building Meaningful Relationships: The foundation of effective mentorship lies in building meaningful and trusting relationships with students. Taking the time to understand each student's strengths, challenges, and aspirations creates a connection that goes beyond the classroom.

Providing Academic Guidance: Mentorship involves academic guidance, helping students navigate their educational journey. This includes assistance with course selection, study strategies, and setting academic goals. A mentor can offer insights into potential career paths and the necessary educational steps to achieve those goals.

Fostering Personal Development: Beyond academics, mentors play a crucial role in fostering personal development. They can provide guidance on developing essential life skills, such as time management, communication, and resilience. Sharing personal experiences and lessons learned contributes to a well-rounded mentorship.

Setting and Monitoring Goals: Effective mentors assist students in setting both short-term and long-term goals. Regularly monitoring progress, celebrating achievements, and providing constructive feedback help students stay on track and motivated.

Being a Role Model: Educators serve as powerful role models for their students. Modeling positive behaviors, values, and a strong work ethic contributes significantly to the mentorship relationship. Students often look up to their mentors as examples of what they can aspire to become.

Creating a Supportive Environment: A key aspect of mentorship is creating a supportive environment where students feel comfortable expressing their concerns and seeking guidance. An open and non-judgmental atmosphere encourages students to discuss challenges they may be facing.

Encouraging Critical Thinking: Mentorship involves encouraging students to think critically and independently. Providing opportunities for discussions, debates, and critical analysis helps students develop essential cognitive skills that extend beyond the classroom.

Promoting Self-Advocacy: Effective mentors empower students to become advocates for themselves. Teaching them how to articulate their needs, seek resources, and overcome obstacles enhances their ability to navigate challenges independently.

In summary, mentorship is a dynamic and multifaceted relationship that goes beyond traditional teaching roles. By actively engaging in mentorship, educators contribute significantly to the holistic development of their students, leaving a lasting and positive impact that extends far beyond the classroom.

Teachers tailor their approaches to diverse student needs

Teachers play a pivotal role in inspiring and meeting the diverse needs of their students. To tailor their approaches effectively, educators can employ a range of strategies that go beyond a one-size-fits-all model. Here are key considerations and actionable steps to inspire different types of learners and cater to diverse student needs:

Understanding Student Diversity: Begin by gaining a deep understanding of the diverse backgrounds, learning styles, and abilities within the classroom. Recognize that each student brings a unique set of strengths and challenges.

Differentiating Instruction: Implement differentiated instruction strategies to address various learning styles. This involves adjusting the content, process, and product of learning to accommodate different student needs. For instance, providing varied materials, allowing for flexible groupings, and offering alternative assessments can be effective.

Utilizing Varied Teaching Methods: Incorporate a variety of teaching methods to engage students with different preferences. Some students may thrive in a hands-on, experiential learning environment, while others may benefit from visual aids or technology-assisted instruction.

Personalized Learning Plans: Develop personalized learning plans for students with specific needs or learning challenges. This involves collaborating with special education professionals, utilizing individualized education programs (IEPs), and providing additional support as needed.

Incorporating Technology: Integrate technology into the classroom to enhance learning experiences. Educational apps, interactive software, and online resources can provide personalized learning opportunities, allowing students to progress at their own pace.

Encouraging Student Choice: Foster a sense of autonomy by allowing students to have some choice in their learning. This could involve selecting topics for projects, choosing from a range of assignments, or deciding on collaborative activities.

Cultivating an Inclusive Environment: Promote an inclusive and welcoming classroom environment where all students feel valued and respected. Celebrate diversity through inclusive teaching materials, literature, and classroom discussions.

Regular Communication and Feedback: Maintain open lines of communication with students and encourage them to express their preferences and concerns. Providing regular feedback ensures that adjustments can be made promptly to address evolving needs.

Professional Development: Engage in continuous professional development to stay informed about best practices for catering to diverse student needs. Attend workshops, collaborate with colleagues, and explore innovative teaching methods.

Seeking Guidance Through Prayer: Finally, it is wisely suggested, to seek guidance through prayer. Asking for divine wisdom and clarity in understanding the unique needs of each student can provide a spiritual foundation for tailoring teaching approaches effectively.

By combining these strategies and remaining adaptable, teachers can create an environment that not only inspires different types of learners but also ensures that each student has the opportunity to thrive in their educational journey.

Educators can instill a resilience and a growth mindset in their students

Establishing a foundation of resilience and a growth mindset is crucial for students to navigate challenges and embrace a love for learning. Educators play a pivotal role in cultivating these qualities. Here are specific ways educators can instill a sense of resilience and a growth mindset in their students:

Promote a Positive Learning Environment: Create a classroom culture that values effort, persistence, and positive attitudes. Reinforce the idea that mistakes are opportunities to learn and grow. Foster a supportive community where students feel comfortable taking academic risks.

Teach the Science of the Brain: Introduce students to the concept of neuroplasticity, explaining that the brain can develop and strengthen with effort and practice. Help them understand that intelligence is not fixed but can be expanded through continuous learning and resilience.

Set Realistic Expectations: Encourage students to set realistic, achievable goals. Break down larger tasks into manageable steps, emphasizing progress over perfection. Celebrate small victories to reinforce the idea that improvement is a continuous process.

Model Resilient Behavior: Demonstrate resilience by sharing personal stories of overcoming challenges. Model a growth mindset by showcasing your own willingness to learn and adapt. Students often draw inspiration from educators who exhibit perseverance.

Provide Constructive Feedback: Offer feedback that focuses on effort, strategies, and improvement rather than fixed abilities. Guide students in understanding that feedback is a valuable tool for growth. Encourage them to view challenges as opportunities to refine their skills.

Integrate Growth Mindset Literature: Incorporate literature and stories that highlight characters facing adversity and overcoming challenges through perseverance and a growth mindset. Discuss these narratives to inspire discussions about resilience.

Encourage Reflection: Incorporate reflection exercises into lessons, prompting students to think about their learning journey. Ask questions that encourage self-awareness, such as 'What did you learn from this experience?' or 'How can you approach this differently next time?'

Foster a Sense of Purpose: Help students connect their learning to a broader purpose. When they understand the significance of their efforts, they are more likely to persevere through challenges. Discuss the real-world applications of their skills and knowledge.

Emphasize the Power of 'Yet': Encourage the use of the word 'yet' in students' vocabulary. When faced with a challenge, teach them to say, 'I haven't mastered this YET.' This simple shift promotes the idea that continuous learning leads to eventual success.

Celebrate Growth and Effort: Acknowledge and celebrate the effort students invest in their learning. Create a system that recognizes improvement, perseverance, and a positive attitude. This reinforces the value of hard work and resilience.

By incorporating these strategies into their teaching practices, educators can contribute significantly to fostering resilience and a growth mindset in their students, preparing them for future challenges with confidence and determination.

.

Addressing challenges or setbacks for success?

Addressing challenges and setbacks is an integral part of a student's journey, and as educators, our role extends beyond academic instruction. While prayer is a powerful component, a holistic approach that combines spiritual guidance with practical strategies can better equip students to navigate difficulties. Here's a more comprehensive perspective:

Prayer as a Foundation: Start by acknowledging the importance of prayer. It provides a foundation for strength, guidance, and resilience. Encourage students to cultivate a habit of seeking spiritual support during challenging times.

Open Communication: Create an environment where students feel comfortable discussing their challenges openly. Foster trust and communication, assuring them that setbacks are a natural part of growth. Be an empathetic listener, understanding their concerns.

Goal Setting and Planning: Work with students to set realistic goals and create actionable plans. Break down larger objectives into smaller, manageable tasks. This approach helps them see the progression of their efforts and minimizes the impact of setbacks.

Teach Problem-Solving Skills: Empower students with problem-solving skills. Guide them in analyzing challenges, identifying potential solutions, and implementing action plans. This cultivates a proactive mindset and a sense of control over their circumstances.

Celebrate Small Wins: Acknowledge and celebrate small victories along the way. Whether overcoming a specific obstacle or achieving a minor milestone, recognizing these successes fosters a positive outlook and motivates students to persevere.

Provide Constructive Feedback: Offer feedback that is constructive and focuses on improvement. Guide students in understanding that setbacks are opportunities to learn and grow. Encourage a mindset that values the process of learning overachieving perfection.

Emphasize the Learning Journey: Shift the focus from grades or outcomes to the learning journey itself. Help students understand that setbacks are part of the educational process and offer valuable lessons. Emphasize the importance of continuous learning and development.

Mentorship and Peer Support: Facilitate mentorship programs or encourage peer support. Sometimes, guidance from a mentor or encouragement from peers who have faced similar challenges can provide invaluable insights and motivation.

Counseling Resources: Connect students with counseling resources within the school or community. Professional guidance can offer additional perspectives and coping strategies for handling setbacks, both academically and personally.

Promote a Growth Mindset: Foster a growth mindset that perceives challenges as opportunities for growth. Teach students that setbacks don't define their capabilities but serve as steppingstones toward success. Encourage resilience and a positive attitude.

By combining prayer with practical strategies and a supportive learning environment, educators can effectively address challenges and setbacks, instilling in students the confidence and determination to strive for success.

Maintaining a healthy balance between challenging students

Maintaining a delicate equilibrium between challenging students and offering the support they require is a nuanced aspect of effective teaching. Striking this balance is crucial for fostering both academic growth and personal development. Consider the following strategies for achieving a harmonious equilibrium:

Individualized Approach: Recognize the unique strengths and weaknesses of each student. Tailor your approach to challenge them in areas where they excel while providing additional support in areas that may be more challenging. This individualized strategy acknowledges the diversity of learning styles within the classroom.

Clear Expectations: Establish clear expectations from the outset. Communicate academic standards and behavioral expectations, ensuring that students understand the criteria for success. Clarity helps create a structured environment where challenges are perceived as benchmarks for improvement rather than obstacles.

Differentiated Instruction: Implement differentiated instruction techniques to cater to diverse learning needs. Provide advanced materials for those who crave additional challenges and offer supplementary resources or extra guidance for those who require additional support. This inclusive approach ensures that all students are appropriately challenged.

Encourage Critical Thinking: Foster a classroom culture that encourages critical thinking. Pose thought-provoking questions, assign projects that require problem-solving, and create an atmosphere where students are inspired to explore beyond the conventional curriculum. This approach challenges students intellectually and promotes a love for learning.

Feedback and Reflection: Establish a feedback loop that includes constructive criticism and positive reinforcement. Regularly discuss students' progress, highlighting their accomplishments and areas for improvement. Encourage self-reflection, empowering students to identify their strengths and weaknesses, fostering accountability in their learning journey.

Flexibility in Assessment: Adopt a flexible approach to assessment. Offer a variety of assessment methods that allow students to showcase their understanding in diverse ways. This flexibility accommodates different learning preferences and ensures that students are both challenged and supported in their assessments.

Promote a Growth Mindset: Instill a growth mindset that perceives challenges as opportunities for learning. Emphasize the process of overcoming difficulties and the importance of resilience. Create an environment where setbacks are viewed as integral to the learning journey, motivating students to persist through challenges.

Open Lines of Communication: Maintain open lines of communication with students. Regularly check in on their well-being, both academically and personally. Actively listen to their concerns, offering guidance and support when needed. This creates a supportive atmosphere where students feel comfortable seeking help.

Collaborative Learning: Encourage collaborative learning experiences. Group activities and projects provide an opportunity for students to challenge each other, share diverse perspectives, and offer support within the peer group. Collaboration fosters a sense of collective achievement.

Professional Development: Continuously invest in your own professional development. Stay informed about evolving teaching methodologies, educational technologies, and strategies for addressing diverse learning needs. This ongoing commitment equips you to better challenge and support your students.

By integrating these strategies, educators can maintain a healthy balance between challenging students and providing the necessary support, creating an enriching and empowering educational experience for all.

Scriptures that support educator's role in making a lasting impact on students' lives.

Proverbs 1:5 (NIV): "Let the wise listen and add to their learning, and let the discerning get guidance."

Philippians 4:13 (NIV): "I can do all this through him who gives me strength."

Jeremiah 29:11 (NIV): "For I know the plans I have for you, declares the Lord, plans for welfare and not for evil, to give you a future and a hope."

2 Timothy 2:15 (NIV): "Do your best to present yourself to God as one approved, a worker who does not need to be ashamed and who correctly handles the word of truth."

Psalm 32:8 (NIV): "I will instruct you and teach you in the way you should go; I will counsel you with my loving eye on you."

Proverbs 16:3 (NIV): "Commit to the Lord whatever you do, and he will establish your plans."

Colossians 3:23 (NIV): "Whatever you do, work at it with all your heart, as working for the Lord, not for human masters."

Matthew 5:16 (NIV): "In the same way, let your light shine before others, that they may see your good deeds and glorify your Father in heaven."

Psalm 119:105 (NIV): "Your word is a lamp for my feet, a light on my path."

Proverbs 22:6 (NIV): "Start children off on the way they should go, and even when they are old, they will not turn from it."

CHAPTER 8:

Overcoming Personal Hardships: Relying on Faith in Difficult Times

Facing personal challenges outside the classroom,

In my journey, I encountered numerous instances where the demands of life outside the classroom collided with professional obligations, creating a profound sense of frustration. One particularly challenging scenario involved simultaneous family obligations and pressing deadlines that seemed insurmountable. The struggle to focus on both aspects left me at a crossroads, grappling with the weight of decision-making.

Amidst this turmoil, I turned to prayer as a sanctuary for guidance and solace. The intersection of family responsibilities and professional commitments presented a dilemma that, with human capabilities alone, seemed impossible to resolve promptly and effectively. It was in these moments that the theoretical knowledge and training I had acquired paled in comparison to the profound impact of divine intervention.

Each plea to the Holy Spirit became a lifeline, a source of strength beyond the realms of conventional problem-solving. It was through this spiritual connection that I found the clarity and resilience to navigate the intricate web of challenges. Faith became the catalyst for solutions, a force that transcended the boundaries of logic and training.

These experiences underscored the transformative power of relying on faith in difficult times, offering not just resolution but a profound sense of connection to something greater than us. In the intricate dance between personal and professional spheres, faith emerged as the unwavering anchor, providing the strength needed to overcome the seemingly insurmountable.

Maintaining a healthy work-life balance while navigating personal hardships,

In the demanding realm of education, maintaining a healthy work-life balance becomes a formidable challenge, especially when personal hardships come knocking. The toll it takes on mental health is often underestimated, impacting not only our well-being but also our effectiveness in the classroom. It's crucial to acknowledge that teachers, like everyone else, grapple with real-life issues while carrying the responsibility of shaping young minds.

In the face of these hardships, faith emerges as the cornerstone for finding balance. I've personally navigated challenges, whether they were financial struggles or the weight of everyday problems that threaten to overshadow our ability to teach. When bills pile up, and the resources seem insufficient, it becomes a moment to turn to prayer.

I vividly recall instances when, enveloped by the uncertainty of financial constraints, I sought solace in prayer, drawing inspiration from the biblical narrative of the Hebrews in exile. Their journey, guided and provided for by God, becomes a powerful metaphor for our own struggles. Through God's grace, protection, and guidance, problems find resolution, and a path forward unveils itself.

Faith isn't just a spiritual anchor; it's a practical guide to weathering the storms of life. It's in those moments of vulnerability that we realize the interconnectedness of personal hardships and professional responsibilities. Faith doesn't magically erase the challenges, but it provides the strength and clarity needed to confront them. It becomes the conduit through which we align ourselves with God's plan, finding resilience and purpose during adversity.

So, in the intricate dance of work and life, faith is the rhythm that keeps us in balance, allowing us to face each day with renewed strength and unwavering commitment to our calling.

Struggling with personal challenges?

In times of personal struggle encroaching on our professional lives, the advice I earnestly offer to fellow teachers is rooted in the transformative power of prayer. Let prayer become not just a ritual but a lifeline, a constant conversation with the Divine that permeates your day.

Begin your morning with prayer, seeking guidance and strength for the challenges that may unfold. Midway through the day, take a moment to reconnect with that source of peace and clarity. And as the day concludes, let prayer be the anchor that steadies your soul.

In the vortex of personal trials, the efficacy of prayer goes beyond mere reassurance. It becomes a source of solace, a reminder that, even during chaos, there exists a force greater than our challenges. The act of prayer, irrespective of one's religious beliefs, taps into a reservoir of positivity, instilling hope, and tranquility.

To those who may question the relevance of faith, consider it not as a dogma but as a conduit for positivity and resilience. Whether you call it God, the Universe, or a higher power, embracing a positive force brings a sense of purpose and calmness.

I've navigated myriad situations through prayer, witnessing its profound impact on my ability to surmount problems. The key is not to reserve prayer for moments of crisis but to weave it into the fabric of your daily routine, fostering a continuous connection with the spiritual realm.

So, as you face personal challenges, don't perceive prayer as a last resort; make it a daily practice, a proactive engagement with the divine. It's not about waiting for adversity to test your faith; it's about nurturing that faith in the serenity of settled times, building a reservoir of strength that will sustain you through life's unpredictable.

Navigating personal hardships

There are many people that have had hardships but one that comes to mind is shared by <u>Reverend Dr. Sandra Baker-Wilson</u>. She says: "I emerged as an overcomer, navigating the harrowing challenges of child molestation and later facing the grim specter of domestic violence as a wife. These were tumultuous chapters in my life, testing the limits of my resilience and faith. In those moments of despair, I turned to Jesus Christ, finding solace and strength in my unwavering trust in the Lord.

The journey through such profound hardships was not easy, but through the lens of faith, I discovered an enduring wellspring of courage and hope. It is my fervent prayer that sharing my testimony can serve as a beacon of light for others facing their own tribulations. Hardships, as the word suggests, are indeed 'hard' to overcome, yet as teachers, we are called to anchor our trust in the Lord.

In the crucible of adversity, my faith in God emerged as the linchpin to my triumph. Every trial became an opportunity to lean on the unwavering support of the Almighty. I give all the praise, honor, and glory to God for being the cornerstone of my resilience.

This testimony is not just a personal narrative; it's a testament to the transformative power of faith. As educators, we are not immune to life's trials, but in trusting the Lord, we find a reservoir of strength that transcends our human limitations.

May my journey inspire others to turn to their faith in times of darkness, recognizing that, through the grace of God, we can emerge not just as survivors but as overcomers. The key to triumph lies in the unwavering belief that, with God, all things are possible."

How can teachers draw strength and resilience
from their faith?

In moments of personal crisis, teachers can unearth reservoirs of strength and resilience by turning to their faith, seeking solace, and understanding from Jesus Christ. Our faith is not a solitary journey but a communal one, and connecting with fellow believers amplifies our ability to weather the storms.

In the depths of despair, it's crucial for teachers to actively engage with their belief in God and the wisdom found in the written word. Turning to scriptures, prayer, and meditation can provide the guidance needed to navigate personal challenges. The transformative power of faith lies not just in professing belief but in actively seeking spiritual nourishment.

Moreover, the strength drawn from our individual faith is fortified when we connect with a supportive community of believers. In times of weakness, fellow believers become pillars of support, offering encouragement, understanding, and shared wisdom. This interconnectedness creates a network of resilience that empowers teachers to persevere.

As educators, our ability to continue effectively in the classroom is intrinsically linked to our spiritual well-being. By actively engaging with our faith, seeking support from fellow believers, and drawing inspiration from the teachings, we can tap into a wellspring of strength that transcends personal crises. Our faith is not just a foundation but a dynamic source of resilience, guiding us through challenges and enabling us to emerge not just unscathed but fortified by the grace of God.

Spiritual practices or rituals for teachers during difficult times

During challenging times, incorporating specific spiritual practices and rituals into your life can serve as a source of solace and strength. One highly recommended practice is regular attendance at a place of worship, such as your local church, where you can engage in communal prayer, seek guidance from spiritual leaders, and find support within a like-minded community.

Fellowshipping with others is a powerful ritual that can create a robust support system. By connecting with fellow believers, you cultivate a network of understanding and compassion. These relationships become a source of encouragement when your spirits are low and offer uplifting companionship when you need it most.

In addition to attending church, consider establishing a personal ritual of daily prayer and reflection. Taking moments each day to connect with your faith, whether through scripture reading, meditation, or personal prayer, can provide a sense of peace and guidance. The Bible encourages us to surround ourselves with godly people, and this can extend to both communal worship and personal spiritual practices.

By actively incorporating these spiritual rituals into your life, you create a foundation of resilience. The transformative power of prayer, coupled with the support of a spiritual community, forms a potent antidote to the challenges life may throw your way. In the embrace of these practices, you'll find not just solace but the strength to overcome and emerge with renewed purpose.

Creating an environment for educators facing personal hardships

Administrators and colleagues play a pivotal role in cultivating environments that foster empathy and support for educators facing personal hardships. I had the privilege of witnessing an inspiring example during my time as a teacher in Nashua, NH, where Ann Wagner, serving as the Special Education Chair, became a vessel for God's grace in remarkable ways.

Ann, along with several dedicated teachers, took a proactive step to address the immediate needs of those going through personal hardships. Recognizing the challenges faced by members of the school community, they established a food pantry. This wasn't just a service for teachers; it extended its embrace to students and staff alike. The initiative became a beacon of support, ensuring that no one within the school community went without essential sustenance.

Ann Wagner's leadership demonstrated that, through God's grace, there is always an abundance of resources when the intention is rooted in compassion. The food pantry became a testament to the windows of heaven pouring out blessings, manifesting in the generosity of donations and the unwavering support of the community.

To create environments that resonate with empathy and support, administrators and colleagues can draw inspiration from such initiatives. Establishing tangible support systems, like a food pantry, not only addresses immediate needs but also symbolizes a community's commitment to standing together through difficult times. By channeling the spirit of compassion, we can manifest God's grace and ensure that no member of the educational community feels alone in their personal struggles.

Strategies for maintaining a positive and hopeful outlook during adversity?

Maintaining a positive and hopeful outlook, even in the face of adversity, is a challenge that many educators encounter. In navigating personal hardships, it's crucial to adopt strategies that go beyond mere acknowledgment of adversity. Here are some actionable recommendations to cultivate resilience and hope through God's grace:

Prayer and Reflection: Start and end your day with prayer and moments of reflection. This spiritual practice not only connects you with a higher power but also provides a space for introspection, allowing you to find strength and guidance.

Community Support: Surround yourself with a supportive community. Share your challenges with trusted colleagues, friends, or mentors who share your faith. A sense of community can offer encouragement, empathy, and the reassurance that you're not facing difficulties alone.

Gratitude Journaling: Keep a gratitude journal where you can document moments of joy, success, and blessings, no matter how small. Focusing on the positive aspects of your life, even amid challenges, helps shift your perspective and cultivates a hopeful outlook.

Mindfulness and Meditation: Incorporate mindfulness and meditation practices into your routine. Taking moments of stillness allows you to center yourself, find peace, and connect with a sense of purpose beyond the immediate challenges.

Set Realistic Goals: Break down larger challenges into smaller, manageable goals. Setting realistic and achievable targets creates a sense of accomplishment and progress, contributing to a positive mindset.

Seek Professional Help: If the challenges seem overwhelming, don't hesitate to seek professional support, whether through counseling, therapy, or pastoral care. Recognizing the importance of mental health and seeking help when needed is a proactive step toward overcoming adversity.

By integrating these strategies into your daily life, you can navigate personal hardships with a positive and hopeful outlook. Remember, through God's grace, there is always a path to overcoming adversity and emerging stronger on the other side.

Leveraging faith to overcome personal challenges

As educators, our faith serves as a powerful anchor in the storm of personal challenges, providing strength and resilience. However, leveraging our faith goes beyond personal endurance; it's about transforming those challenges into opportunities for empathy and connection with our students.

Personal Testimonies: Share your personal testimonies with students. Open-up about your own struggles, highlighting how your faith played a pivotal role in overcoming adversity. Authenticity breeds connection, and students may find comfort and inspiration in knowing that their teacher faced challenges too.

Incorporate Faith in Lessons: Integrate faith-based lessons or discussions into the curriculum, where relevant. This allows students to see the practical application of faith in navigating real-life challenges. Use literature, historical events, or current affairs to explore themes of resilience, hope, and faith.

Create a Safe Space: Foster a classroom environment where students feel safe to share their struggles. Emphasize that challenges are a part of life and that, just as you rely on your faith, they can find strength in their beliefs. Encourage dialogue and provide support without judgment.

Mentorship and Guidance: Offer mentorship grounded in faith. Actively listen to students, providing guidance through the lens of your own experiences. This connection can be transformative, as students see a role model who not only talks about faith but lives it.

Prayer Circles: Establish prayer circles within the school community. This can be a forum for both educators and students (if in a private school setting) to come together, share intentions, and offer prayers of support. It creates a sense of solidarity and interconnectedness.

Service Projects: Engage in faith-inspired service projects. Demonstrate compassion in action by organizing initiatives that address community needs. This hands-on approach to faith reinforces the values of empathy, kindness, and service.

Remember, leveraging faith is not just a personal journey; it's a communal one that extends to the students we guide. By actively incorporating our faith into our educational roles, we create an environment where resilience, empathy, and connection flourish.

Scriptures that support Overcoming Personal Hardships: Relying on Faith in Difficult Times

Isaiah 41:10 (NIV): "So do not fear, for I am with you; do not be dismayed, for I am your God. I will strengthen you and help you; I will uphold you with my righteous right hand."

Psalm 34:18 (NIV): "The Lord is close to the brokenhearted and saves those who are crushed in spirit."

Philippians 4:13 (NIV): "I can do all this through him who gives me strength."

2 Corinthians 1:3-4 (NIV): "Praise be to the God and Father of our Lord Jesus Christ, the Father of compassion and the God of all comfort, who comforts us in all our troubles, so that we can comfort those in any trouble with the comfort we ourselves receive from God."

Psalm 46:1 (NIV): "God is our refuge and strength, an ever-present help in trouble."

Matthew 11:28-30 (NIV): "Come to me, all you who are weary and burdened, and I will give you rest. Take my yoke upon you and learn from me, for I am gentle and humble in heart, and you will find rest for your souls. For my yoke is easy and my burden is light."

Romans 8:28 (NIV): "And we know that in all things God works for the good of those who love him, who have been called according to his purpose."

Psalm 23:1-4 (NIV): "The Lord is my shepherd, I lack nothing. He makes me lie down in green pastures, he leads me beside quiet waters, he refreshes my soul. He guides me along the right paths for his name's sake. Even though I walk through the darkest valley, I will fear no evil, for you are with me; your rod and your staff, they comfort me."

James 1:12 (NIV): "Blessed is the one who perseveres under trial because, having stood the test, that person will receive the crown of life that the Lord has promised to those who love him."

Psalm 55:22 (NIV): "Cast your cares on the Lord and he will sustain you; he will never let the righteous be shaken."

These scriptures can provide a foundation for discussing the role of faith in overcoming personal hardships, offering solace and encouragement to those facing challenges.

CHAPTER 9:

Hallelujah Moments: Celebrating Successes and Milestones

My Hallelujah moment

I vividly recall my 'Hallelujah moment' in my teaching career when I earned my master's degree in education. This achievement wasn't just a personal triumph but a testament to the divine guidance that shaped my journey. I faced financial constraints earlier, and it took two decades for the circumstances to align, allowing me to pursue and complete my master's degree. In that moment, I felt a profound confirmation that teaching was not just my profession but a divine calling.

Another jubilant moment occurred 15 years later when I became an ordained minister and attained a doctorate degree in Christian Counseling. These milestones were undeniably the handiwork of God, and I attribute all my accomplishments to His grace. The journey to these achievements was marked by challenges and perseverance, but the 'Hallelujah moments' made every trial worthwhile.

In celebrating your achievements as educators, I encourage you to embrace the significance of each milestone. Here are a few ways to make your celebration meaningful:

Reflection and Gratitude: Take a moment to reflect on your journey. Express gratitude for the challenges you've overcome and the growth you've experienced. Acknowledge the divine guidance that played a role in your success.

Share Your Story: Don't hesitate to share your story with colleagues and students. Your journey can inspire and motivate others. Be transparent about the obstacles you faced and the resilience that propelled you forward.

Communal Celebration: Organize a communal celebration within your school community. Whether it's a small gathering or a recognition ceremony, sharing your achievements with peers fosters a sense of camaraderie and mutual support.

Set New Goals: Use your 'Hallelujah moment' as a steppingstone. Reflect on new goals and aspirations, aligning them with your calling as an educator. The celebration becomes a launchpad for continued growth and contribution.

Express Your Faith: If faith is a cornerstone in your life, consider incorporating expressions of faith into your celebration. A prayer of gratitude or a moment of reflection can add a spiritual dimension to the occasion.

Remember, each achievement, no matter how big or small, deserves recognition. Celebrate not just the destination but the journey, appreciating the divine guidance that shapes us.

Milestones or achievements that educators may overlook,

Becoming a teacher is undoubtedly a significant milestone in one's life, signifying the profound responsibility and privilege of positively impacting others. While this is a notable achievement, there are several other milestones and accomplishments that educators may overlook in the course of their careers. Recognizing and celebrating these moments is crucial for fostering a sense of accomplishment and motivation. Here are some common milestones that educators may not always acknowledge:

Individual Student Achievements: Take note of the achievements of your students, both big and small. It could be a struggling student mastering a challenging concept or a shy student gaining confidence. Celebrate these moments as they reflect the impact of your teaching on individual lives.

Innovative Teaching Approaches: If you experiment with new teaching methods or integrate innovative approaches into your lessons, consider it a milestone. Embracing change and adapting your teaching style shows professional growth and a commitment to providing the best learning experience.

Positive Classroom Culture: Creating a positive and inclusive classroom culture is an ongoing achievement. Acknowledge moments where students feel supported, engaged, and motivated to learn. These instances contribute to a nurturing environment for both educators and students.

Professional Development: Completing workshops, courses, or certifications may go unnoticed. However, these are valuable milestones that enhance your skills and knowledge. Take the time to recognize and celebrate your commitment to continuous professional development.

Impact on School Community: Whether you organize extracurricular activities, mentor colleagues, or contribute to the school community, recognize your role beyond the classroom. Your positive influence on the broader educational environment is a noteworthy achievement.

To learn to recognize and celebrate these moments effectively:

Keep a Journal: Maintain a journal to document daily successes, positive interactions, and notable achievements. Reflecting on these entries regularly can help you appreciate your journey.

Peer Recognition: Encourage a culture of peer recognition within your school. Celebrate each other's successes during staff meetings or through a dedicated platform where educators can share accomplishments.

Set Personal Goals: Establish achievable personal goals for your teaching practice. When you attain these goals, take the time to acknowledge and celebrate the progress you've made.

Celebrate as a Team: Create a supportive environment where educators celebrate each other's milestones. Collaborative celebrations build a sense of community and shared success.

By acknowledging these often-overlooked milestones and embracing a culture of celebration, educators can derive inspiration, motivation, and a renewed sense of purpose in their noble profession.

Celebrating successes contribute to a positive and motivating school culture,

Celebrating successes is not merely a formality; it is a powerful catalyst that significantly contributes to fostering a positive and motivating school culture for both educators and students. Recognizing and commemorating achievements creates a ripple effect that permeates the entire educational community. Here's how such celebrations play a pivotal role:

Fosters a Sense of Pride and Accomplishment: When educators and students are acknowledged for their achievements, it instills a sense of pride and accomplishment. This positive reinforcement boosts self-esteem and motivates individuals to strive for excellence in their future endeavors.

Strengthens Community Bonds: Celebrations bring people together, creating a shared experience that strengthens the bonds within the school community. Whether it's a teacher's innovative teaching method or a student's academic breakthrough, shared celebrations build a supportive network that encourages collaboration and camaraderie.

Promotes a Growth Mindset: Recognizing successes, no matter how small, contributes to cultivating a growth mindset. Both educators and students learn to perceive challenges as opportunities for growth and improvement. This mindset shift is fundamental for creating a culture that values continuous learning and resilience.

Inspires and Motivates: Celebrating successes serves as a source of inspiration and motivation. Educators witnessing the achievements of their peers are motivated to explore innovative teaching methods, while students are inspired by the accomplishments of their fellow learners. This positive cycle of motivation fuels a dynamic and forward-thinking educational environment.

Sets a Positive Tone: Regular celebrations set a positive tone within the school culture. A culture that emphasizes acknowledging and appreciating achievements creates an optimistic atmosphere where individuals feel valued and recognized. This positivity becomes a driving force that permeates every aspect of the school's daily life.

Encourages Goal Setting: Celebrations provide an opportunity to reflect on past achievements and set new goals. By highlighting what has been accomplished, educators and students can collectively establish future objectives, fostering a sense of purpose and direction.

Enhances School Reputation: A school that actively celebrates successes builds a positive reputation within the broader community. This reputation attracts talented educators, engaged students, and supportive parents, contributing to the overall success and vibrancy of the educational institution.

Celebrating successes is not merely a formality, but a cornerstone for creating a thriving, positive, and motivating school culture. It propels individuals to reach their full potential, nurtures a supportive community, and sets the stage for continuous growth and success.

How the celebration of achievements positively impact teacher morale

In my extensive experience in the field of education, I have witnessed firsthand the profound positive impact that the celebration of achievements can have on teacher morale and job satisfaction. Teachers, entrusted with a myriad of responsibilities, often find themselves navigating a demanding and dynamic environment. The celebration of achievements serves as a beacon of encouragement, fostering a range of benefits that contribute to their overall well-being.

For instance, during a school-wide recognition ceremony, I observed the genuine joy and sense of accomplishment radiating from teachers who were acknowledged for their innovative teaching methods, outstanding contributions to the curriculum, or successful engagement initiatives. These celebrations not only validated their hard work but also served as a powerful morale booster.

The positive impact on teacher morale is particularly evident when achievements are acknowledged in a manner that goes beyond routine appreciation. Personalized recognitions, such as highlighting specific accomplishments in newsletters, school assemblies, or staff meetings, demonstrate a sincere acknowledgment of individual efforts. This level of recognition not only elevates teacher morale but also reinforces their belief in the value of their contributions.

Moreover, celebrating achievements contributes to a more positive and collaborative working environment. Teachers feel a sense of camaraderie when they witness and celebrate each other's successes. This collective celebration not only enhances the overall morale within the teaching community but also fosters a collaborative spirit that positively influences job satisfaction.

Job satisfaction is further enhanced when the celebration of achievements is integrated into the school's culture as a regular practice. A school environment that prioritizes recognizing and celebrating accomplishments cultivates a positive ethos where teachers feel appreciated and motivated. This, in turn, has a direct correlation with job satisfaction, as teachers are more likely to derive fulfillment from their roles when their efforts are acknowledged and celebrated.

In summary, the celebration of achievements serves as a potent catalyst for uplifting teacher morale and enhancing job satisfaction. By creating a culture that values and celebrates the accomplishments of educators, we not only acknowledge their hard work but also contribute to the creation of a positive and rewarding professional environment.

Strategies or rituals recommended for educators to acknowledge their achievements,

Absolutely, celebrating achievements, regardless of their size, is crucial for maintaining a positive and motivated teaching community. Here are some specific strategies and rituals that educators can adopt to acknowledge and commemorate their achievements:

Create a Recognition Board: Establish a dedicated board or wall space in a common area where educators can pin notes, achievements, or photos showcasing their successes. This serves as a visual reminder of individual and collective accomplishments.

Monthly Celebrations: Designate a specific day each month to celebrate achievements. This could be done during a staff meeting or through a brief gathering. Recognize teachers who have achieved milestones, completed successful projects, or demonstrated exceptional dedication.

Peer-to-Peer Recognition: Encourage a culture of peer-to-peer acknowledgment. Set up a system where teachers can nominate their colleagues for outstanding efforts or achievements. This not only boosts morale but also fosters a sense of camaraderie.

Personal Reflection Journals: Provide educators with personal reflection journals. In these journals, teachers can document their daily or weekly achievements, no matter how small. Encourage them to revisit these entries during challenging times for a positive mindset.

Professional Development Celebrations: Acknowledge teachers' commitment to continuous learning and professional development. Celebrate the completion of workshops, certifications, or other educational milestones, emphasizing the value of lifelong learning.

Ceremonial Events: Organize periodic ceremonial events to commemorate major achievements. This could include an annual awards ceremony, where educators are recognized for their dedication, innovation, or years of service.

Gratitude Circles: Initiate gratitude circles during staff meetings. Allow teachers to express gratitude for their colleagues' support, share success stories, and acknowledge the positive impact of teamwork.

Social Media Shoutouts: Leverage social media platforms to celebrate achievements. Share success stories, photos, or highlights of educators' accomplishments. This not only celebrates individuals but also promotes a positive image of the school community.

Wellness Retreats: Consider organizing wellness retreats or team-building activities. These events provide an opportunity for educators to relax, bond, and reflect on their achievements in a more informal setting.

Mentorship Recognition: Establish a mentorship program and recognize mentors and mentees for their contributions. Celebrate the growth and achievements resulting from mentorship connections.

Remember, the key is to make celebration a consistent and integral part of the school culture. By adopting these strategies, educators can create a supportive and uplifting environment that fosters continuous growth and positive morale.

School leaders can play a role in fostering a culture of celebration

Administrators play a pivotal role in shaping the culture of celebration and recognition within a school. Here are some specific strategies they can implement to foster a culture of appreciation among the teaching staff:

Establish a Recognition Program: Create a formal recognition program that includes categories such as Teacher of the Month, Most Innovative Lesson Plan, or Collaborator of the Quarter. Develop clear criteria and involve both teachers and students in the nomination process.

Regular Celebratory Events: Organize regular celebratory events, such as monthly staff meetings dedicated to acknowledging achievements. During these events, administrators can publicly recognize teachers who have demonstrated excellence, reached milestones, or contributed significantly to the school community.

Peer-Nominated Awards: Introduce awards that are peer-nominated. Allow teachers to nominate their colleagues for specific accomplishments or acts of support. This not only encourages positive collaboration but also ensures that recognition comes from those who understand the daily challenges teachers face.

Feature Success Stories: Create a platform, whether through newsletters, school websites, or bulletin boards, to feature success stories of teachers. Highlight their achievements, innovative teaching methods, or positive impacts on students. This can inspire others and create a sense of pride within the school.

Student Recommendations: Involve students in the recognition process by asking them to recommend teachers who have made a positive impact on their learning experience. This not only provides genuine feedback but also strengthens the teacher-student relationship.

Professional Development Acknowledgement:
Acknowledge teachers who actively engage in professional development. Celebrate certifications,

workshops attended, or academic advancements. This emphasizes the school's commitment to continuous learning and growth.

Surprise Celebrations: Organize surprise celebrations for individual teachers or the entire staff. This could include small parties, luncheons, or even moments of acknowledgment during school assemblies. The element of surprise adds an extra layer of excitement.

Create a Recognition Wall: Designate a physical space within the school, such as a recognition wall, where achievements, commendations, and appreciative notes can be displayed. This provides a constant visual reminder of the collective successes of the teaching staff.

Personalized Tokens of Appreciation: Provide personalized tokens of appreciation, such as certificates, plaques, or small gifts, to teachers on special occasions or when they achieve notable milestones. This adds a tangible element to the recognition.

Encourage Team Celebrations: Foster a sense of camaraderie by encouraging departments or grade-level teams to celebrate their collective achievements.

This promotes teamwork and collaboration among teachers.

By implementing these strategies, administrators can contribute to a positive and motivating school culture where teachers feel valued and recognized for their contributions.

Feel hesitant or uncomfortable celebrating your own successes?

Teachers, it's essential to recognize and celebrate the unique talents and successes that God has bestowed upon you. Embracing your achievements not only uplifts your spirit but also inspires those around you. If you find yourself hesitating or feeling uncomfortable about celebrating your own successes, consider the following advice:

Gratitude and Humility: Remember that celebrating your successes doesn't diminish humility; instead, it allows you to express gratitude for the gifts and abilities you've been given.

225

Recognizing your achievements is a way of acknowledging the divine blessings that contribute to your effectiveness as an educator.

Share the Glory: Consider framing your success as a collective achievement. Acknowledge the support, collaboration, and guidance you've received from colleagues, students, and mentors. This approach reflects the interconnected nature of success in the teaching profession.

Impact on Others: Reflect on the positive impact your success has on others, especially your students. Celebrating your achievements sets an example for them, demonstrating the value of hard work, dedication, and acknowledging one's accomplishments. It can inspire them to strive for their own greatness.

Professional Growth: Viewing celebrations as markers of professional growth can make the process more comfortable. Recognize that each success, no matter how small, contributes to your ongoing development as an educator. This perspective shifts the focus from self-promotion to continuous improvement.

Create a Supportive Environment: Foster a school culture that encourages and celebrates individual and collective achievements. When the entire school community embraces a culture of acknowledgment, teachers may find it more natural to participate in celebrating their successes.

Set Personal Milestones: Establish personal milestones and celebrate them as part of your professional journey. Whether it's mastering a new teaching technique, completing professional development, or receiving positive feedback from students, these milestones deserve acknowledgment and celebration.

Connect with Colleagues: Engage with colleagues who have experienced similar feelings. Share your hesitations and learn from their experiences. Sometimes, discussing these emotions openly can help normalize the act of celebrating one's successes.

Celebrate Quietly, If Needed: If grand celebrations feel uncomfortable, find quieter ways to mark your achievements. This could be through personal reflections, expressions of gratitude, or even small gestures of self-appreciation.

Remember, celebrating your successes is not about self-promotion but about recognizing and appreciating the talents and contributions you bring to the educational journey. By embracing your successes, you contribute to a positive and uplifting environment that benefits both you and those around you.

Creating a supportive environment where colleagues celebrate each other's accomplishments,

Educators play a pivotal role in fostering a supportive environment where colleagues genuinely celebrate each other's accomplishments and share in each other's successes. Here are some practical strategies to make this collaborative culture thrive:

Cultivate a Culture of Openness: Encourage open communication and transparency among colleagues. Create a culture where sharing successes is welcomed and celebrated, not seen as bragging. Establish regular forums, such as team meetings or professional development sessions, where teachers can share their achievements, big or small.

Recognition Platforms: Implement a recognition platform, whether it's a bulletin board in the staff room, a dedicated section in newsletters, or a digital platform, to highlight and celebrate individual and team accomplishments. Consider organizing regular award ceremonies or appreciation events where educators can be formally recognized for their contributions.

Peer-to-Peer Acknowledgment: Encourage teachers to acknowledge and celebrate each other's successes directly. This can be done through congratulatory emails, personalized notes, or shout-outs during meetings. Establish a peer-to-peer recognition program where educators nominate colleagues for their outstanding efforts, and the recognized individuals receive public acknowledgment.

Collaborative Projects: Foster a collaborative spirit by encouraging educators to work together on projects. When a project succeeds, celebrate it collectively as a shared achievement. Recognize and showcase collaborative efforts in achieving specific goals, whether they relate to student outcomes, innovative teaching methods, or community engagement.

Shared Professional Development: Facilitate opportunities for teachers to share their expertise through workshops, presentations, or collaborative professional development sessions. Recognize educators who contribute significantly to the professional growth of their colleagues, creating a culture of continuous learning and collaboration.

Celebratory Rituals: Establish celebratory rituals, such as a monthly 'Success Friday' where educators share their achievements over a casual gathering. Encourage small team celebrations for milestones achieved, providing a sense of camaraderie and shared accomplishment.

Leadership Role Modeling: School leaders should lead by example. Share your successes and challenges with the staff, creating a culture where everyone feels comfortable doing the same. Model collaborative behavior by recognizing and celebrating achievements at all levels within the school community.

Remember, creating a supportive environment requires a collective effort. When educators are open, supportive, and genuinely excited about each other's successes, it contributes to a positive school culture that benefits everyone.

The role of reflection in the celebration of successes,

Reflection plays a crucial role in the celebration of successes, serving as a powerful tool for educators to deepen the impact of their achievements. Here's how educators can leverage reflection to amplify the significance of their successes:

Intentional Self-Reflection: Encourage educators to engage in intentional self-reflection after accomplishing a goal or milestone. Ask questions like, 'What worked well?' and 'What challenges did I overcome?' This process allows teachers to gain insights into their strengths and areas for growth.

Identifying Growth Opportunities: Use reflection as a means to identify areas for growth even in successful endeavors. What could be improved or done differently next time? This forward-thinking approach turns successes into continuous learning opportunities.

Connecting Successes to Goals: Have educators connect their successes to broader personal or professional goals. Reflection should include an examination of how the achievement aligns with their overarching objectives, fostering a sense of purpose and direction.

Celebrating Collaborative Achievements: For collaborative achievements, reflection becomes a shared experience. Facilitate team reflections where educators collectively discuss the journey, share individual perspectives, and highlight the collaborative efforts that contributed to success.

Documenting Achievements: Encourage educators to document their achievements and reflections. This could be in the form of a journal, a digital platform, or a shared space within the school. Documenting success helps educators track their progress and provides a tangible record of their growth.

Expressing Gratitude: Reflection should include a moment of gratitude. Educators can reflect on the support received from colleagues, administrators, or students. Expressing gratitude not only enhances the joy of success but also strengthens interpersonal connections within the school community.

Sharing Success Stories: Actively promote the sharing of success stories during professional development sessions or staff meetings. Educators can take turns sharing their reflections, creating a positive and uplifting atmosphere that inspires others.

Professional Development Planning: Use reflection to inform future professional development plans. What skills or knowledge did the success highlight? How can educators further develop these areas to enhance their teaching practice?

By incorporating reflection into the celebration of successes, educators not only acknowledge their achievements but also engage in a continuous process of growth and improvement. This intentional approach transforms successes into catalysts for ongoing professional development and collaboration.

Scriptures That support Hallelujah Moments:
Celebrating Success and Milestones

Psalm 118:24 (NIV): "The Lord has done it this very day; let us rejoice today and be glad."

1 Thessalonians 5:16-18 (NIV): "Rejoice always, pray continually, give thanks in all circumstances; for this is God's will for you in Christ Jesus."

Psalm 105:1 (NIV): "Give praise to the Lord, proclaim his name; make known among the nations what he has done."

Psalm 34:1 (NIV): "I will extol the Lord at all times; his praise will always be on my lips."

Philippians 4:4 (NIV): "Rejoice in the Lord always. I will say it again: Rejoice!"

Colossians 3:15-17 (NIV): "Let the peace of Christ rule in your hearts, since as members of one body you were called to peace. And be thankful. Let the message of Christ dwell among you richly as you teach and admonish one another with all wisdom through psalms, hymns, and songs from the Spirit, singing to God with gratitude in your hearts. And whatever you do, whether in word or deed, do it all in the name of the Lord Jesus, giving thanks to God the Father through him."

Psalm 150:1-6 (NIV): "Praise the Lord. Praise God in his sanctuary; praise him in his mighty heavens. Praise him for his acts of power; praise him for his surpassing greatness. Praise him with the sounding of the trumpet, praise him with the harp and lyre, praise him with timbrel and dancing, praise him with the strings and pipe, praise him with the clash of cymbals, praise him with resounding cymbals. Let everything that has breath praise the Lord. Praise the Lord."

James 1:17 (NIV): "Every good and perfect gift is from above, coming down from the Father of the heavenly lights, who does not change like shifting shadows."

Psalm 103:2-5 (NIV): "Praise the Lord, my soul, and forget not all his benefits—who forgives all your sins and heals all your diseases, who redeems your life from the pit and crowns you with love and compassion, who satisfies your desires with good things so that your youth is renewed like the eagle's."

Psalm 136:1 (NIV): "Give thanks to the Lord, for he is good. His love endures forever."

These scriptures can serve as a foundation for discussing the biblical perspective on celebrating success and milestones, emphasizing gratitude, praise, and the acknowledgment of God's goodness.

CHAPTER 10:

A Lifelong Journey: Continuing to Grow as an Educator and Person

Approaching and prioritizing ongoing professional development

I approach and prioritize ongoing professional development in my teaching career with a strategic and purposeful mindset. Attending seminars and workshops serves as an invaluable opportunity to glean insights and strategies that align with my teaching philosophy. I conscientiously evaluate the applicability of each concept to the unique needs of my students, fostering a dynamic and responsive learning environment.

My commitment extends beyond the classroom walls, emphasizing collaboration and open communication with students, parents, administrators, and fellow colleagues. I view professional development not only as an individual endeavor but as a collective journey, where shared insights and diverse perspectives enrich the educational landscape.

By incorporating the most impactful strategies into my teaching style, I aim to create an inclusive and engaging atmosphere that resonates with the audience I serve. This approach ensures that my ongoing development directly translates into tangible benefits for the learning experiences of my students.

My professional growth is intertwined with my dedication to enhancing the educational journey of those under my guidance. The dynamic interplay of evolving strategies, collaboration, and effective communication propels my commitment to lifelong learning and continuous improvement in the realm of education.

Examples of where learning and growth impacted teaching and personal well-being

Over the course of my teaching career, which spans seven different states and eight school districts, I've had the privilege of encountering a diverse array of educational environments and administrative structures. This extensive journey has been intrinsically linked with continuous learning and professional growth, and the symbiotic relationship between teaching and training has been a cornerstone of my development.

Allow me to illustrate this with a few concrete examples. In one instance, my exposure to a progressive teaching methodology during a specialized workshop reshaped my approach to student engagement. The incorporation of interactive strategies not only invigorated my classroom dynamics but also contributed to a more enriching learning experience for my students.

Additionally, navigating various administrative landscapes has been a continual learning process. Each encounter with different leadership styles and organizational structures has imparted valuable insights into effective communication, adaptability, and collaborative problem-solving. These lessons have, in turn, influenced my teaching practice by fostering a more holistic and responsive approach.

The impact of this ongoing learning extends beyond the professional realm, significantly contributing to my personal well-being. As I embrace new methodologies, educational philosophies, and administrative frameworks, a sense of fulfillment and purpose permeates my journey. The joy derived from witnessing positive changes in my students' learning experiences and the continuous refinement of my skills reinforces my commitment to both professional growth and personal well-being.

The interconnected nature of teaching and learning has not only enriched my pedagogical approach but has also become an integral source of personal satisfaction and well-being throughout my lifelong journey as an educator.

Maintaining a growth mindset contributes to ongoing development,

In the ever-evolving landscape of education, maintaining a growth mindset is paramount for educators seeking continual development. However, I firmly believe that, alongside cultivating a growth mindset, knowing Jesus and incorporating faith into one's teaching philosophy are equally indispensable. These elements synergistically contribute to a holistic approach to education.

A growth mindset is transformative in its ability to fuel resilience, adaptability, and a passion for learning. Educators embracing this mindset view challenges not as insurmountable obstacles but as opportunities for growth. They understand that setbacks are steppingstones to improvement, and this outlook permeates every aspect of their teaching practice.

Yet, the incorporation of faith adds a profound layer to the educator's journey. Recognizing the divine purpose in each student and acknowledging the responsibility bestowed upon teachers by God enhances the meaning and significance of our calling. It instills a sense of purpose and a commitment to nurturing not just academic growth but also the spiritual and personal development of our students.

To foster this dual mindset throughout their careers, educators can engage in intentional practices. Regular reflection on teaching experiences, both successes and challenges, allows for continuous improvement and aligns with the principles of a growth mindset. Simultaneously, prayer and seeking guidance from spiritual mentors contribute to the development of a faith-based perspective in teaching.

Practical strategies include creating a supportive community of educators who share similar values and beliefs. This community can serve as a source of encouragement, shared wisdom, and collective prayer. Additionally, incorporating faith-based principles into classroom rituals, discussions, and decision-making processes creates an environment where both growth and spirituality are nurtured.

The dynamic interplay of a growth mindset and faith not only fosters personal and professional development but also elevates the impact educators can have on the lives of their students. It transforms teaching into a calling—a sacred journey of continuous learning, improvement, and spiritual enrichment.

Faith role in shaping your journey

My faith plays an integral role in shaping my ongoing journey of personal and professional development as an educator. It serves as the bedrock of my commitment to acquiring knowledge, not only in my content area of education but also through formal training in theology. This dual pursuit allows me to seamlessly integrate discussions on curriculum and spirituality, illustrating how the intersection of both realms can profoundly impact teaching.

Through my faith, I find inspiration and a deep-seated motivation to delve into the intricacies of education and theology. It is this symbiotic relationship that has propelled me to acquire the necessary tools to articulate the profound connection between curriculum and spirituality. The knowledge gained empowers me to not only educate minds but also nurture the spirits of my students, fostering a holistic approach to teaching.

Believing that my faith has been instrumental in bringing me this far, I recognize the shaping and preparation that God has orchestrated throughout my journey. Every challenge, every milestone, and every moment of growth has been guided by the divine hand. My faith has been the compass, guiding me through the complexities of education and spirituality, reinforcing my commitment to the calling of teaching.

As I reflect on my journey, I am compelled to share the strength and resilience that my faith has instilled in me. It serves as a testament to the transformative power of intertwining personal spirituality with professional development. Through my faith, I have been shaped into an educator with a purpose—to motivate and support Christian teachers, assuring them that they are not alone in their journey.

My faith isn't just a facet of my life; it is the driving force behind my actions, my commitment to continuous learning, and my dedication to uplifting those around me. It is this unwavering faith that emboldens me to navigate the ever-evolving landscape of education, confident that God's guidance will continue to shape and illuminate my path.

Advice for teachers feeling overwhelmed

The advice I offer to fellow teachers facing moments of overwhelming stress or stagnation is rooted in the profound reasons that brought you into this noble profession. It's crucial not to lose sight of the initial passion and purpose that ignited your journey into teaching. When faced with challenges, it's easy to forget the impact you can have on young minds and the lives you can shape.

Remember, you are not alone in this endeavor. Forge connections with other educators who share similar experiences and can offer valuable insights. Collaborating with colleagues can provide a supportive network where ideas are exchanged, and collective wisdom thrives. Additionally, seek connections beyond the classroom—engage with your church community, draw inspiration from scriptures, and most importantly, connect with God.

In moments of overwhelm, it's essential to embrace the belief that calling on the name of the Lord is not just a remedy but a transformative source of guidance. God, in His infinite wisdom, can illuminate your path and lead you to the right direction. Teaching, though immensely rewarding, is not without its challenges. It's during these low moments that knowing how to recharge becomes paramount.

Consider these challenging moments not as setbacks but as opportunities for growth and renewal. Reflect on the impact you've had and the lives you've touched. Let the nobility of your calling as an educator rekindle the passion for learning and teaching. Embrace the truth that, through the grace of God, you possess the strength to overcome challenges, reignite your passion, and continue the sacred calling of shaping minds and hearts.

My advice is a call to reconnect with the intrinsic motivations that led you to become an educator, foster meaningful connections, draw inspiration from your faith, and trust in the divine guidance that can navigate you through the complexities of the teaching profession. Remember, you are part of a community that shares the commitment to education and the profound impact it has on the future.

Incorporating faith enhanced teaching effectiveness and personal fulfillment

Certainly, there are numerous instances in my teaching career where incorporating faith into professional development activities has not only enhanced my effectiveness as an educator but has also brought personal fulfillment. One notable example is the integration of biblical principles into curriculum development.

During a professional development session on curriculum enhancement, I drew inspiration from biblical teachings to infuse ethical and moral dimensions into the content. This not only provided a unique perspective for my students but also fostered a learning environment that emphasized values such as compassion, integrity, and empathy.

Another instance involves utilizing prayer as a foundational element in classroom management strategies. Recognizing the significance of creating a positive and respectful atmosphere, I incorporated prayer as a daily ritual to set a tone of gratitude and unity among students. This simple yet profound practice has contributed to a more harmonious classroom dynamic and improved student-teacher relationships.

Furthermore, engaging in collaborative learning with colleagues has been enriched by incorporating faith-based principles. During group discussions on effective teaching methods, we often draw parallels between our faith values and teaching philosophies. This shared understanding has not only strengthened our professional bonds but has also provided a source of encouragement and support in navigating the challenges of education.

These examples illustrate how intertwining faith with professional development activities has a transformative impact on teaching effectiveness and personal fulfillment. It goes beyond theoretical frameworks, enriching the educational experience with values that resonate on a deeper level. By aligning professional growth with faith-based principles, the journey of personal and professional development becomes more purposeful and spiritually rewarding.

Professional development plan that aligns with career goals and spiritual growth?

Absolutely, creating a personalized professional development plan that aligns with both career goals and spiritual growth is a thoughtful and intentional process.

To guide this endeavor effectively, consider the following steps:

Self-Reflection: Begin by reflecting on your current strengths, areas for improvement, and the alignment of your teaching philosophy with your spiritual beliefs. Identify specific aspects of your career and spiritual journey that you wish to enhance.

Set Clear Goals: Define clear, measurable, and achievable goals for both your career and spiritual growth. For example, in your teaching career, you might set a goal to integrate faith-based values into a specific curriculum. Simultaneously, for spiritual growth, you could set a goal to deepen your understanding of how your faith intersects with education.

Research and Resources: Explore literature and resources that bridge the gap between career development and spiritual enrichment. Look for books, articles, or workshops that specifically address integrating faith into education. This could include topics such as moral education, character development, or teaching strategies aligned with spiritual principles.

Networking and Mentorship: Connect with like-minded educators who share your commitment to both professional excellence and spiritual growth. Seek mentorship from individuals who have successfully navigated this intersection. Their insights and experiences can provide valuable guidance.

Professional Development Opportunities: Attend conferences, workshops, or training sessions that offer a blend of career-focused and spiritually enriching content. Look for events that explicitly address the integration of faith and teaching methodologies. These opportunities can contribute significantly to your growth on both fronts.

Regular Reflection and Adjustment: Periodically revisit your professional development plan to assess progress. Reflect on how the integration of spiritual principles has impacted your teaching and personal life. Be open to adjustments and refinements as your journey unfolds.

Incorporate Spiritual Practices: Integrate spiritual practices into your daily routine. This could involve prayer, meditation, or moments of reflection. Connecting with your faith regularly can provide a foundation for resilience and inspiration in your teaching career.

Remember, the key is to approach professional development and spiritual growth holistically, recognizing the interconnectedness of these aspects in your teaching journey.

Scriptures that support A Lifelong Journey: Continuing to Grow as an Educator and Person

Proverbs 4:7 (NIV): "The beginning of wisdom is this: Get wisdom. Though it cost all you have, get understanding."

Philippians 3:13-14 (NIV): "Brothers and sisters, I do not consider myself yet to have taken hold of it. But one thing I do: Forgetting what is behind and straining toward what is ahead, I press on toward the goal to win the prize for which God has called me heavenward in Christ Jesus."

2 Peter 3:18 (NIV): "But grow in the grace and knowledge of our Lord and Savior Jesus Christ. To him be glory both now and forever! Amen."

Colossians 2:6-7 (NIV): "So then, just as you received Christ Jesus as Lord, continue to live your lives in him, rooted and built up in him, strengthened in the faith as you were taught, and overflowing with thankfulness."

Proverbs 3:5-6 (NIV): "Trust in the Lord with all your heart and lean not on your own understanding; in all your ways submit to him, and he will make your paths straight."

Jeremiah 29:11 (NIV): "For I know the plans I have for you, declares the Lord, plans for welfare and not for evil, to give you a future and a hope."

Psalm 119:105 (NIV): "Your word is a lamp for my feet, a light on my path."

Ephesians 4:22-24 (NIV): "You were taught, with regard to your former way of life, to put off your old self, which is being corrupted by its deceitful desires;

to be made new in the attitude of your minds; and to put on the new self, created to be like God in true righteousness and holiness."

Proverbs 16:3 (NIV): "Commit to the Lord whatever you do, and he will establish your plans."

Colossians 1:10 (NIV): "So that you may live a life worthy of the Lord and please him in every way: bearing fruit in every good work, growing in the knowledge of God."

These scriptures can serve as a foundation for discussing the lifelong journey of personal and professional growth, emphasizing the importance of seeking wisdom, staying rooted in faith, and continually striving toward personal and spiritual development.

In the Christian Bible, there are several verses that refer to the calling of teachers and preachers by God. One such verse is found in the New Testament book of Ephesians, chapter 4, verse 11-12 which says:

"So, Christ himself gave the apostles, the prophets, the evangelists, the pastors and teachers, to equip his people for works of service, so that the body of Christ may be built up."

This passage suggests that those who hold positions of leadership and teaching in the church are called and equipped by God to guide and instruct the faithful. The reference to the "body of Christ" refers to the community of believers, and the role of teachers and preachers is to help each member of this community grow in faith and serve others.

There are also numerous stories in the Bible that illustrate the importance of teaching and preaching. For example, in the Old Testament book of Exodus, God calls Moses to lead the Israelites out of slavery in Egypt and instructs him to pass on the teachings and commandments of God to the people. In the New Testament, Jesus himself is often referred to as a teacher and preacher, as he traveled throughout the region teaching and spreading his message of love and compassion.

Overall, the Bible emphasizes the importance of teachers and preachers in guiding and nurturing the spiritual growth of believers and suggests that those who are called to these roles have been given a special gift from God.

AND………

For my Muslim teachers, yes, there are several verses in the Quran that emphasize the importance of teachers and preachers in Islam. Here are some of them:

"Allah will exalt in degree those of you who believe, and those who have been granted knowledge. And Allah is Well-Acquainted with what you do." (Quran 58:11)

"Allah raises those who believe among you, and those who have knowledge, to high ranks." (Quran 58:11)

"O you who have believed, fear Allah and seek the means [of nearness] to Him and strive in His cause that you may succeed." (Quran 5:35)

"And [mention, O Muhammad], when Allah took a covenant from those who were given the Scripture, [saying], "You must make it clear to the people and not conceal it." But they threw it away behind their backs and exchanged it for a small price. And wretched is that which they purchased." (Quran 3:187)

These verses emphasize the importance of seeking knowledge, the value of those who have been granted knowledge, and the obligation of teachers and preachers to share that knowledge with others.

In addition to these verses, Prophet Muhammad (peace be upon him) also emphasized the importance of seeking knowledge and the role of teachers in Islam. He said: "Seeking knowledge is obligatory upon every Muslim." (Sunan Ibn Majah 224)

Prophet Muhammad also emphasized the status of teachers in Islam, saying: "The best among you are those who learn the Quran and teach it." (Sahih Al-Bukhari 5027)

In Islam, the position of a teacher is highly respected and valued, and seeking knowledge is considered an important part of a Muslim's life.

Regardless of the faith we follow, whether it be Christianity or Islam, the divine call upon teachers remains universal. As you reflect on the inspirational narratives within this book, may the moments of praise and gratitude transcend religious boundaries, encompassing the diverse experiences of educators worldwide.

May the wisdom shared by these dedicated teachers resonate deeply with your own journey, serving as a source of inspiration and guidance. Their testimonies stand as a testament to the profound impact educators can have on the lives of their students.

In closing, let this be a collective celebration of the teaching profession, a recognition of the challenges overcome, and a moment to express gratitude for the successes achieved. As you continue your teaching endeavors, may these stories be a constant reminder that, through dedication and faith, every educator plays a vital role in shaping the future.

May the lessons shared in this book linger in your heart, guiding your path with resilience and purpose. Let us give glory to God for the success of these teachers and for the impact you, too, will undoubtedly make in the lives of those you teach.

May your teaching journey be blessed, purposeful, and filled with hallelujah moments. Here's to the unwavering commitment of educators around the world. May God's grace continue to illuminate your path and the path of every teacher who strives to make a difference.

About the Author

Dr. Anthony Dayse is a highly seasoned public-school educator, devoting his life to the transformative power of teaching and inspiration. He has taught in 6 different states. His fervor for education is seamlessly woven with his deep-rooted love for the Lord, shaping both his professional endeavors and written works.

Bringing over three decades of experience as a K-12 public-school teacher, College Instructor and mentor, Dr. Dayse has emerged as a compelling advocate, uplifting educators worldwide. As an ordained minister, holding a doctorate in Christian Counseling and a master's in education, he possesses a profound comprehension of the subject matter, enabling him to articulate intricate ideas with clarity and precision. Through his written contributions, Dr. Dayse shares rich insights, personal experiences, and pragmatic advice, aiming to empower teachers at every level and encouraging them to discover joy and purpose in their vocation.

Married to his lifelong sweetheart Maribel and blessed with two children, Dr. Dayse's personal and professional life reflects a harmonious blend of faith, commitment, and familial love. His unwavering dedication to his work has positioned him as a potent advocate for educators worldwide, championing their needs and acknowledging their invaluable contributions. Dr. Dayse's written works serve as a beacon, inspiring teachers to recognize the profound significance of their role and embrace both the challenges and joys inherent in their calling.

In conclusion, Dr. Dayse's wealth of experience, unyielding passion, and steadfast commitment render him an invaluable resource and a wellspring of inspiration for educators, parents, and students alike.

www.ingramcontent.com/pod-product-compliance
Lightning Source LLC
Chambersburg PA
CBHW060910120626
46553CB00001B/273